WALKING IN NORTHUMBERLAND

Warkworth Castle above the Coquet (Walk 35)

WALKING IN NORTHUMBERLAND

by

Alan Hall

CICERONE PRESS
MILNTHORPE, CUMBRIA

ISBN 1 85284 265 2
A catalogue record for this book is available from the British Library.

To Hector

ACKNOWLEDGEMENTS

This Northumbrian journey of rediscovery renewed old friendships and made new ones, not only with the land but with those who live and work throughout the county. For no matter where help and encouragement were needed it was graciously given and gratefully received, even though on occasions the greeting was classic Northumbrian, "Whae ya bugger, y'ar back agaen!"

I must record my thanks for the help and encouragement from Catriona Mulligan and John Steel of Northumberland National Park; Jonathan Farries of Forest Enterprise, Rothbury Forest District; Bill Burlton and Penny of Forest Enterprise, Kielder Forest; Chris Pringle of Northumbrian Water; Ian Turvey of The National Trust, Wallington and the County Council Rights of Way Office. Equally essential and appreciated was the co-operation of landowners, farmers and shepherds who kept me on the straight and narrow.

My final words of thanks are for my backroom team of Greta and Hector, suppliers of ever ready expertise in matters grammatical and graphic, and Roberta Carruthers for her illustrations.

All photographs and maps are by the author, illustrations are by Roberta Carruthers, and poems and verse carry their author's name if known.

Other Cicerone titles by the same author:

The Border Country - A walker's guide
Border Pubs & Inns - A walker's guide
Walks in the Lammermuirs - A walker's guide

Front Cover: Salter's Nick and Shaftoe Crags (Walk 20)

CONTENTS

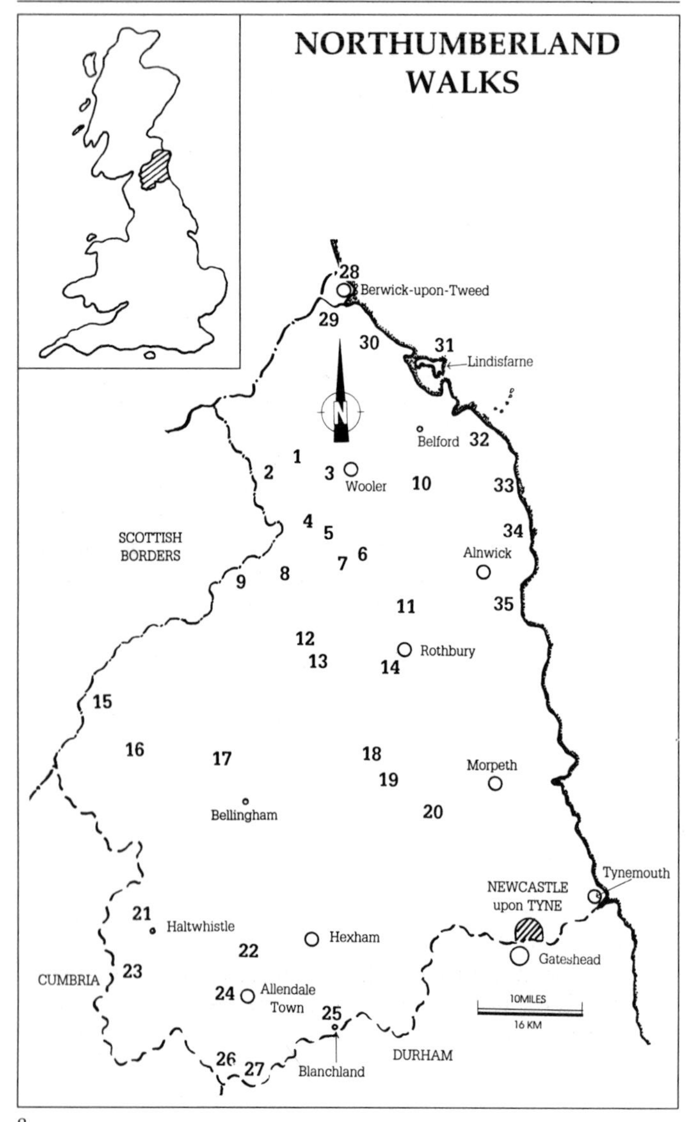
NORTHUMBERLAND
WALKS
28
Berwick-upon-Tweed
29
30
31
Lindisfarne
N
Belford
32
1
2
3
Wooler
10
33
4
5
34
SCOTTISH
BORDERS
6
7
Alnwick
9
8
11
35
12
Rothbury
13
14
15
16
17
18
Morpeth
19
Bellingham
20
Tynemouth
NEWCASTLE
upon TYNE
21
Haltwhistle
Hexham
22
Gateshead
CUMBRIA
23
24
Allendale
Town
25
10MILES
16 KM
26
27
Blanchland
DURHAM

INTRODUCTION
Background

NORTHUMBERLAND

Provinciae omnes Northymbryorum

The crowning county of England - yes, the best!
Have you and I, then, raced across its moors
A.C. Swinburne, *The Sisters*

Roman inability to subdue the rebellious Picts and Scots and extend their empire in and around AD 81, was in many ways instrumental not only in the conception but also the birth of Northumberland as a frontier region. For when their great Wall was abandoned at the end of the fourth century and they retreated to their dwindling empire, the Romans left the land to a volatile mix of Celtic tribes. This wild and lonely, history and blood soaked, land continued for the next sixteen centuries in a pulsating mix of violence and peace, family feuds, Christian conversion, agrarian reform and forest decimation.

The Northumberland we see today, a much smaller land mass than Northumbria, was created in AD 1080, not by the inhabitants of Northumbria but by invading Scots who defeated the Northumbrians at Carham by the River Tweed. The victors declared that all lands lying between Tweed and Tyne were to be named 'Northumberland'.

Northumberland is an extensive county that rises and ripples to wide horizons, where space and solitude are in abundance and time is measured by the seasonal cycle. Unusual rugged lands with a population to match, like no other in the UK, with perhaps the exception of the Scottish Borders to whom Northumberland is bonded by blood and a shared history. It has remained one of the most sparsely populated in England since the days of the Domesday Book; when one square mile carried but five people, expanding in the thirteenth century only to recede in the fourteenth, to 17 people per square mile. This was principally due to the ravages of the Black

Death, an unstable economy resulting from the Battle of Bannockburn, and the onset of the Border Wars. Change has been slow and memorabilia of conflict still predominates; to quote B Long from *Castles of Northumberland* - 'Northumberland has more castles, fortalices, peles, bastles and barmikins than any other county in the British Isles'.

With the advent of the eighteenth century Northumberland was to experience the extraction, by whatever means, of its rich seams of coal in its south-east corner and lead and silver from its southern dales. Essential, basic raw materials fed the insatiable appetites of the industrial revolution, and with the revolution a new breed of landowners and landlords transformed Northumberland. From the Dukes of Northumberland to coal and lead lessees such as the families of Blackett and Beaumont, estates were transformed, new model villages were constructed, fields drained, stone steadings built, hedges set and plantations raised; in addition to the construction of many miles of new roads and the improvement of old ones. Such activity raised the coal and heavy engineering capital Newcastle to its zenith of industrial achievement, due in no small measure to men such as Lord Armstrong, engineer, inventor and arms manufacturer, who also fathered the grand gesture of Cragside and subsequently fashioned the restoration of Bamburgh Castle.

Bounded by the Tweed to the north, and the Tyne, Derwent and an assortment of dalesheads to the south, with Cumbria binding its western marches and the restless North Sea its eastern flanks, this most northerly of English counties is big in every sense. With some 2020 square miles, the fifth largest county in England, its rural population is however as sparse as any. Only 10 per cent of the total population dwell outside the south-east corner of Tyneside's industrial triangle; the one time heartland of the Northumbrian coalfield and the Tyne's shipyards, cradle of the *Mauretania* and *Queen Elizabeth* 2 - alas no more.

Excluding the City of Newcastle-upon-Tyne and the urban conglomeration of Tyneside there are few townships of any size in the county. Berwick-upon-Tweed, much fought over, Alnwick, the county town, Morpeth, seat of the county council, Hexham with its stately abbey, the old lead mining centre of Allendale Town, and Rothbury, capital of Coquetdale, all have a character of their own with much to offer the walker.

The majority of the county's acres are still privately owned and managed, with 398 square miles (1031sq km), of the wildest and most remote areas under the guardianship of The Northumberland National Park, one of eleven within England and Wales. Granted National Park status in 1956 the Park authorities have been working to maintain the essential character of the county. Traditional farming practices are encouraged and support is given for the conservation of natural and semi-natural habitats, whilst introducing wild, scenically attractive areas to the general public by improving amenities and wildlife conservation. There exists today, within the National Park, a network of accessible public and permissive paths, thanks in no small measure to the unceasing efforts and enthusiasm of the Park's Public Rights of Way Officers.

Within the Park's perimeters there are vast tracts, mainly in North Tynedale, owned by the Forestry Commission, who hold one-fifth of the total area, as do the Ministry of Defence above Otterburn and Redesdale.

The Forestry Commission created, from 1926, Kielder Forest, Britain's largest forested area of 60,000 hectares, of which some 50,000 hectares are planted, yielding 400,000 cubic metres annually for the construction industry, particleboard and paper making. Within the forest area floats Europe's largest man-made lake, Kielder Water Reservoir, holding 44,000 million gallons (200,000 million litres) of water in an area of 2800 acres (1335 hectares), 7½ miles (12km) in length and a shoreline in excess of 27 miles (43.2km). Both Forest Enterprise and Northumbrian Water have provided amenities and encourage all lovers of the great outdoors.

The Ministry of Defence (MOD), who own Otterburn and Redesdale Training Area, occupy 58,000 acres of moorland wilderness and at the time of writing are wanting more. The announcement of their intentions not surprisingly brought forth a clamour of angry voices, not least among them the National Park. A Public Enquiry is being held and if the military men of Whitehall have their way by the time this guide is published the perimeter Red Flags of the MOD will have extended and Northumberland's wilderness may not be so quiet.

Although such is a thorn in the county's side let us not lose sight of the fact that Northumberland provides some of the best unfettered hill, dale and coastal walking in Britain.

CLIMATE AND WEATHER PATTERNS

As with all areas in this temperate island Northumberland's climate is affected by its position in relation to the prevailing south-west Atlantic winds. Situated on the north-eastern perimeter of England it is generally regarded by many, as North Tynedale was once described, as 'cool, wet and windy'. A misconception, for although mountainous and moorland for large areas, the county is subject to fewer severe snowstorms or sustained winter frosts than its northern and western counterparts, and rarely do wind speeds exceed 50mph. Its rainfall is less than half that deposited on the popular playgrounds of the English Lakes and the Scottish Highlands.

Sunshine and Temperature

Experience indicates that May, June and July enjoy the longest hours of sunshine with a daily average of 5 to 6 hours along the coast, coastal belt and in sheltered dales. As hours of sunshine and temperature are affected, to a certain extent, by the height above sea level conditions above 1000ft (305m) are not quite so benign with sunshine levels and temperatures correspondingly lower.

Figures point to July as the warmest month with daily coastal temperatures averaging from 10.5°C - 19.5°C, and January the coldest month with a daily average of 5.8°C maximum and 0°C minimum. To estimate higher ground temperatures use the simple 'Lapse Rate' calculation, i.e. a reduction of 3°C for every 1000ft (305m) in height above sea level. June to September in all parts of Northumberland are shown to be the warmest months.

Precipitation

Controlled by the prevailing wind, the time of year and the height above sea level the areas of most rainfall are in the west and north of the county. Here the western Cheviots and the hills of North Tynedale receive an annual rainfall of 50 inches while the eastern Cheviots (including The Cheviot massif) attracts only 45 inches; and the Pennine fells above the Allendales receiving approximately 50 inches. Lowland areas of Northumberland, from the coast to the dales' floors and lower slopes, receive by contrast annual quantities between 27 inches to 35 inches with the driest months of the year being March, April and June; the wettest in summer is August, and the wettest in winter are November, December and January.

During winter months snow very rarely restricts the walker with average coverings enhancing the scene and providing that little extra challenge. January and February are the months when snow lies for approximately 10 days above 1000ft.

Visibility

Rural Northumberland has always enjoyed clear unpolluted air and far-seeing views. Today, with the demise of mineral mining in the Allen Dales and the decline of heavy industry in the county's south-eastern Tyneside triangle, visibility has been enhanced. Night-time fogs are a rare occurrence and invariably clear as temperatures increase during the day. Sea haars lasting most of the day are occasionally experienced, from April to September, and can reduce the pleasure of walks in Chapter 3.

Winds

Wind strength and direction varies depending on the time of year with the county enjoying an annual average at lower levels of winds of 8-10mph. Calm conditions prevail for the majority of the year with 90 per cent of the year's windspeeds bracketed within 1-19 miles (1.6-30km) per hour. The remaining 10 per cent is not so benign, producing the occasional evil gale-force 8 north-easterly; an abrasive wind that can transform a pleasant trek on the high hills into a major expedition.

Such events are fortunately infrequent - the last time a storm-force wind of great ferocity struck Northumberland was over a century ago on Sunday 2 July 1893 in the vicinity of Bloodybush Edge (Walk 8). This furious conflict between earth, wind and water as reported in *The Alnwick Gazette* states 'The Waterspout, the result of a thunderstorm of unrivalled ferocity, riving [scooping] 30 to 40 acres, to a depth of up to 5 feet, of peat from the flanks of Bloodybush Edge'. So violent was the roaring spate 'that many blocks of peat, many tons in weight, were tossed about and piled up into the floor of the valley below. The Waterspout caused this devastation in 1½ hours, during which time the flood of the Breamish rose and fell'.

When to Walk

Past weather patterns indicate that May, June and July provide the brightest, driest conditions for the Northumberland walker with soft winds, agreeable temperatures and long bright days. Although it has been said, by experienced pedestrians, that any time of the year is a good time to walk in Northumberland. For if its moors and mountains are cloaked and cold there are the four-season's alternatives of its golden beaches or riverside paths to enjoy.

FLORA AND FAUNA

Flora

On Northumberland's hills and ridges colourful heathers and bleached grasses dominate. Heathers (*Calluna*) proliferate on the higher ground with bell heather (*Erica*) flourishing on the drier eastern slopes, whilst on the upland prairies indigenous grasses abound and provide the distinctive hallmark for Northumberland's fells. Matgrass, wavy-hair grass and tussocks of purple moor grass monopolise the high plateaux with flourishing bilberry and patches of not so common cloudberry on drier ground. On wetter or sodden high ground several mosses, along with the ever-present sphagnum and cotton grass (*Scotsman's Heid*) provide useful indicators to the walker that wet conditions exist underfoot.

Crags surrounding the upland dales provide an ideal habitat for plants such as thyme and rock rose together with lichens and certain ferns, also an uncertain foothold for several species of old woodland.

Descending lower the ground cover consists of fescues, Yorkshire fog, patches of rushes and ever-increasing areas of duplicitous bracken. Lower still by river bank and valley floor tormentil, vetch, primrose, cowslip, aconite, celandine and canterbury bell, together with orchids on the wetter pastures, brighten the scene.

Primrose

Of the indigenous ancient woodlands that once covered vast areas of the county few examples remain save in isolated cases in secluded cleughs and crags where natural regenerating oak, ash, beech, silver birch, alder, rowan and hazel can occasionally be found. Happily several estates and enlightened foresters are now in the process of recreating these native woodlands, as an alternative to the extensive forest of conifers that cover much of the county today. For within the confines of Kielder Forest and Rothbury Forest District alone there are stands of Sitka spruce and Lodgepole pine of 40,000 hectares and 10,500 hectares respectively; in addition to considerable holdings of privately owned coniferous plantations. Although, today, the regimentation of the 'farmed' conifer is greatly softened by careful and considerate restructuring of the forests and the provision of facilities for wildlife and the public at large.

Salt-laden winds and coastal temperatures govern the flora of Northumberland's 'Lordly Strand', with its miles of sweeping sandy bays and ever-changing delicate dunes. Blackthorn, the tallest shrub to inhabit the shoreline, bends with the wind, whilst thrift, thyme and sea campion shelter at ground level, and the sandy dunes, in addition to hosting the long-rooted binding grasses, are home to sea spurge and the white bells of sea bindweed.

Fauna

Northumberland is a haven of delight for ornithologists, zoologists and entomologists, particularly in spring and early summer when the cycle of life begins. Whether it be on the Cheviot range, the forests of North Tyne Dale, the dark stark moors of wild West Allen Dale or the golden sands of Bamburgh, with over 300 bird species, ranging from eider ducks ('St Cuthbert's Chicks') to the tumbling peewit, inhabiting or passing through the county, the walker is never without sight or sound of these colourful and amusing companions.

Plover

Seasonal departure of many species does not greatly depress the numbers, nor the interest, for migrants out are immediately replaced by visitors in. Grouse, blackcock, partridge, rook, pigeon, heron, many raptors, blackbird, robin and finch, guillemot and gull remain all year; with such as wheeling plovers, swift and swallow, cuckoo and mountain blackbird (ring ouzel) leaving for warmer surrounds to return in the spring. Winter replacements, pink geese, grey lags, snowbuntings and field fares, and vast skeens of wildfowl, visit its shores, particularly the flats and banks of Budle Bay and Lindisfarne. Even the curlew, emblem of the Northumbrian National Park, leaves its moors and fells for the winter comfort of Northumberland's shore.

With few cliffs to speak of the sea birds, puffins, razor bills, shags, guillemots, fulmers and razor bills nest on the rocky Farne Islands. Here a nesting colony of terns have a nasty habit of 'dive-bombing' unwanted visitors who invade their grassy nesting site.

On the open moorlands of the Cheviot range and high northern dales small herds of feral goats roam, with roe deer preferring the quiet cleughs and forest fringes, in company with fox, bounding blue (in winter white) mountain hares, stoats and weasels. In the county's many burns and rivers otters are returning, and unfortunately also the voracious feral mink inhabits these waterways. Grass snakes and the shy but poisonous adder, also favour the warm burnsides in summer. Should an adder bite (its venom is rarely fatal) qualified medical help should be sought immediately.

Of the smaller mammals, newts, toads, frogs and slow-worm, fieldmouse and vole, and a strain of myxametosis-resistant rabbit inhabit the burnside, riverside and loughside haughs and pastures.

Insects in Northumberland are myriad, from the rare northern brown argus butterfly and the more prevalent small copper and common blue, to the colourful dragonflies, pond skaters and beetles, whilst not forgetting the largest sawfly in Britain. Unfortunately, so are the hordes of stinging nasties found in the forests, beside brackish water and upland heather, such as the fells of West Allen Dale, at dawn. Leaders of the pack are the horsefly - 'cleg' - and the female midge, both extremely voracious in humid, windless summer days. The wise

Adder

carry, and apply, an insect repellent; I can recommend any containing Diethyltoluamide - 'Diet' for short.

HISTORY

Physical

TABLE

Time Chart

BC	Significant Events Affecting Northumberland
400,000,000	Devonian Era: Northumberland was born beneath a vast sea ringed by mountain ranges, from where eroded iron oxide - hematite - when washed into the sea, compacted and oxidised into an orange/red rock, Old Red Sandstone, found in north-west Northumberland. Later, volcanic activity produced the igneous rock or granite of the Cheviot range, including the 'Metamorphic Aureole' as seen in the outcrop crags of Cunyan, Hawsen, Housey and Langlee.
280,000,000	Carboniferous Era: An eternity of sedimentation laid down the Cementstones, a group of limestones, sandstones and shales, with further sandstone deposits spread in a wide arc south of the Cheviot granite. Examples of this Fell Sandstone are the Kielder Stane, the Drake Stone and the craggy rims of Simonside and Harbottle. Here subsequent strata tilt produced the inward facing escarpments and outward folding flanks exhibited today. Islands in shallow Carboniferous seas supported primitive plant life, later buried by deposits of lime, sand and mud to create seams of carbon - the Scremerston Coal Group. The era drew to a close as more limestones were deposited over thicker carbon layers, resulting in the rich coalfields of the south-east, and ended with a flurry of violent mountain building. Igneous rocks were heaved and squeezed, with Magma - molten basalt - intruding into the fault lines and fractures, then cooling to form Dolerite - hard whin sill. Later to be used as building stone in Hadrian's Wall and many castles such as Bamburgh and Dunstanburgh.

	In the Allen Dales and South Tyne Dale magma, in association with hot gases and liquids, intruded into faults in the strata, later to cool as mineral bearing veins of lead, silver, zinc, copper, fluorspar and barytes.
2,000,000-12,000	
	The Ice Age: Finally fashioned today's horizons; mountains were ground down and rounded and valleys gouged along the fault lines, whilst, beneath the ice cap, melt water created V-shaped dry valleys. Classic examples are seen in the College and Harthope valleys and the dry valley below Humbleton Hill.
9000	Tundra conditions, when an open ground cover of lichen and moss developed, followed by the intrusion of scrub.
7000	Sea levels rose significantly in the North Sea resulting in the submergence of the continental land-link and the formation of Northumberland's fine coastline.
6000	Deciduous woodlands flourished below mountain height, replacing considerable areas of conifers.
4000	Forest clearing, assisted by a decline of the elm and the hand of man, encouraged ground-hugging vegetation.

Time, wind and water have honed the sculptures of the Ice Age, bestowing upon Northumberland its unmistakable and unique profile.

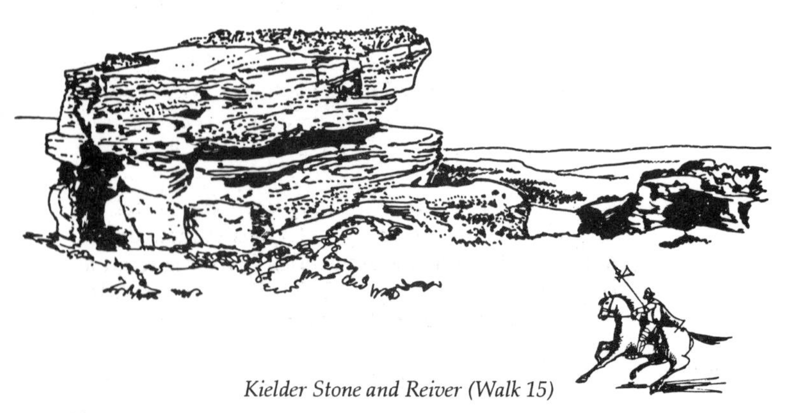

Kielder Stone and Reiver (Walk 15)

Human

TABLE

BC

6000-3500	Mesolithic Man ventured north to reach Northumberland - hunters, fishers and gatherers; they left little behind.
3500-1500	Stone Age man was replaced by Bronze Age man, whose stone circles, tumulae and earth-bound stones abound on the northern fells. Many boulders bear 'Cup and Ring' inscriptions, thought to be connected with matters of birth, life and death.
1500-AD	As the Bronze Age ran into the more advanced Iron Age, around 600 BC, a tribe of Celts, the Votadini, spilled south from southern Scotland; Nothumberland's first historically recorded inhabitants. A restless race of marauders, the precursers of the Reivers, they ranged with their animals over the rough uplands, on which they built simple settlements of wood and earth. Evidence of their settlements and forts litter the Cheviots, Coquetdale and the Breamish valley, the largest crowning Yeavering Bell - a defensive site with extensive views.

AD

75-400	From Tiber to Tyne and Tweed the Roman Legions came, an event that was as dramatic as it was constructive. In their 300 year occupation they were to construct a network of roads, mineral mines and, greatest of all, from AD 112, Hadrian's Wall of stone and earth. From Wallsend to the Solway, a continuous barrier for 80 Roman miles, i.e. 75 miles (120km), built to exclude the fractious Celts and Picts, it gave the county a frontier feel, which in places lingers still. By the end of the fourth century the legions had abandoned the Wall, allowing the indigenous Celts free reign to continue squabbling and feuding and totally unprepared to resist the invading Anglians from northern Europe.
500-1000	Ida, an Anglian king, seized the stony eyrie of Bamburgh

in AD 745, from where the conquest of Northumbria was to radiate. By the end of the sixth century a successor, King Edwin, had established his palace at Old Yeavering and overrun Glendale and the eastern Cheviots. Yet Celtic place names remained - Yeavering, Breamish, Tweed, Kielder and Redesdale - which suggests the Anglian conquest had been relatively bloodless and subsequently symbiotic.

Strong and concerned Northumbrian kings nurtured Anglo-Celtic cultural development and the spread of Christianity by Celtic monks from Lindisfarne. No such concern was extended to the indigenous flora, as the Anglians swept the trees and scrub aside to make way for the plough; a predicament later compounded by the voracious appetites of ewes of the Northumbrian abbeys such as Newminster.

The developing peace was relatively short lived, pounded by waves of pillaging Danes breaking on Northumberland's shores in the eighth century, desecrating Lindisfarne in AD 793. The harbingers of mayhem and destruction that was to continue erupting in Northumberland until well after the Union of the Crowns in 1603.

1000-1600 A cycle of comparative peace followed the Norman Conquest in the eleventh to thirteenth centuries, when the county enjoyed a series of benevolent Earls of Northumberland. Monasteries and priories were built - Newminster and Brinkburn, coupled with an upsurge of castle construction - Warkworth, Dunstanburgh, Alnwick and Bamburgh.

This calm ended with the demise of Alexander III of Scotland in 1285. An event that allowed the greed and aggression of Edward II of England to plunge both sides of the Border into three centuries of endless violence and degradation. Known as the 'Killing Times', when farms were fortified and pele towers rose from every knowe.

To quote R.H. Tawney, 'in Northumberland landlords measure their wealth by the men they can bring out as the summons goes'. Also Robert Newton states in *Tudor Northumberland*, 'the clan chieftains of Redesdale and North Tynedale ruled a society resembling that of the Scottish Highlands'.

1700- Peace and prosperity returned to Northumberland with the Hanovarian eighteenth century, orchestrated by the great estates and fuelled by new money generated by the mining of coal, lead, iron and silver, and the engineering miracle of industrial Tyneside.

Many relics of our predecessors grace Northumberland's landscape. Let not the lessons of centuries past be forgotten in this land of the elongated vowel; eee doon't aah knaa!

COUNTY GUIDELINES

I am greatly in favour of the principle of Country Codes, for are we not beholden to our heritage and our fellows to respect both, and leave behind nothing but our appreciation of the countryside and all that it contains. What I am not in favour of is the dictatorial dictum of the 'Do Not' brigade, no matter what gospel they preach. I would therefore commend to the Northumbrian walker a series of positive guidelines - as produced by the major guardians of Northumberland's natural resources, Northumberland National Park, Forest Enterprise and Northumbrian Water. Respectively they declare their intentions in the 'Curlew Country Code', 'Customer Care Statement' and 'Landscape and Leisure'.

Northumberland National Park 'Curlew Country Code'

Please

- leave gates as you find them
- use stiles and gates to cross walls and fences
- keep to rights of way
- don't disturb or damage wildlife, plants and trees
- take your litter home
- keep all water clean
- guard against risk of fire
- keep all dogs under control, preferably on a lead, particularly at lambing time
- leave livestock, crops and machinery alone

- whether walking, cycling, riding or driving take extra care on country roads
- keep the countryside peaceful for everyone

Rights of Way

You have the right to walk, ride or drive along a path, bridleway or byway according to its status. To assist you and help prevent trespass many rights of way are colour coded,

Yellow for footpaths,
Blue for bridleways,
Red for byways

Public Footpaths -	access for walkers only
Bridleways -	open to walkers, riders and cyclists
Byways -	usually unsurfaced tracks open to walkers, horse riders, cyclists and other vehicles
Permissive Paths -	the use of some additional footpaths has been negotiated with landowners, waymarked accordingly
Open Land -	on most moorland and farmland visitors normally have no automatic right of access without permission from the landowner

The Environment, Safety, Organised Activities and the Park's Code of Conduct are covered in the pamphlet 'Make the Most of Your Visit'.

Forest Enterprise Customer Care Statement

1) Monitor all recreation facilities and services in Kielder and Rothbury Forests on a regular basis
2) Aim to maintain our facilities and services at consistently high standards
3) Investigate any reported fault or complaint, undertake any necessary remedial action
4) Do our utmost to ensure our facilities are open at the time advertised

We Would Ask You Our Visitors To

1) Obey all warning notices, forest operations such as tree felling take place throughout the forest and all year round
2) Take advantage of waymarked trails for walking, cycling and horse riding; they have been chosen because they provide good views and easy access into the forest
3) Park sensibly and do not obstruct barriers or other access points
4) Do everything you can to avoid disturbing wildlife
5) Respect all users of the forest; Kielder has many visitors who engage in a wide variety of recreational pursuits
6) Please let us know if you have any complaints or comments. You can let us know through the visitors book at Kielder Castle or Kielder campsite, or by contacting the Environmental Officer - address and telephone in 'Useful Information'.

The moors and fells of Northumberland instantly indicate to the walker that this is a land of sheep and to a lesser extent grouse. Please respect the property of those who gain their living from these lonely places by ensuring that you keep to the paths, and leave your dog at home during lambing and nesting times, and circumnavigate the grouse moors from 12 August to 12 December.

The Roman Wall east of Great Chesters to Steel Rigg, Hot Bank Crags and Sewingshields Crags (Walk 21)

Action

ACCESS and ACCOMMODATION

Access

Road Links: Situated approximately in the centre of the UK, Northumberland is a forgotten land regarding major approach roads, the Romans and General Wade apparently contributing more than their successors. Although the premier A1(T) Edinburgh to London road passes through the county, there are but a few miles of motorway, the A1(M), by the extremities of industrial Tyneside. Terrain and a violent past have restricted roads running north/ south to the A1(T), A68(T), A697 and the east/west approaches to the A69(T) and A689. Internal A-roads are limited to the A1(T) - Newcastle to Berwick, the A68/A68(T) - Corbridge to Carter Bar, the A696(T) - Newcastle to Otterburn, the A697 - Morpeth to Coldstream, the A69(T) - Newcastle to Carlisle, the A686 - Hexham to Alston and the A689 - Alston to Brampton.

Internal progress to many interesting areas is, more often than not, by tortuous B-roads that favour a north/south route as opposed to an east/west course, a classic example being the 'Coastal Scenic Route'. Such ways have a tendency to hug the lower ground whilst weaving alongside estate boundaries. Several unclassified lanes venture over the fells to link dale with dale, often single track with passing places, yet it is invariably such links that lead to the cream of Northumberland's walks.

John McAdam, the great road pioneer, remarked in 1823, 'The roads of East Allendale are altogether the worst that have come to my knowledge'. Indeed it was not until the mid-1800s that Stephen Oliver noted that a 'road was built by Kielder and Deadwater into Scotland'.

Rail links: One Inter-City, the east coast London-Edinburgh line, passes through the county, stopping at Newcastle-upon-Tyne and Berwick-upon-Tweed. A local stopping 'sprinter service' also utilises this line, with a Newcastle to Carlisle service operating through the Tyne valley.

Bus Services: Long Distance express services from the majority of major cities and towns in England and Scotland stop at Berwick-upon-Tweed, Alnwick, Morpeth, Hexham and Newcastle-upon-Tyne.

Local Services: For such a sparsely populated county it is adequately served by local buses. Several operators, including, at the time of writing, the Royal Mail Postbus, provide transport to and from outlying districts, connecting the Allen Dales, Blanchland, Haltwhistle, Haydon Bridge, Hexham, Redesdale, Rothbury & Coquetdale, Tynedale - North and South - Wooler and surrounds. Hadrian's Wall has its own regular named bus service operating from Hexham and Carlisle.

Free copies of local bus services are available from local bus stations, village post offices, local libraries and tourist information centres. For services in the south of the county the timetable 'Bus & Train Services - Across the Roof of England' is available at every imaginable outlet.

Access by Foot: Northumberland provides infinite acres of space and measureless miles of public paths, bridleways, byways and permissive paths. Many utilise Roman roads, military ways, trade routes, drove roads, carrier's ways, miner's tracks, rail beds and paths from village to mine, church or farm. Many are within the designated areas of the Northumberland National Park, the Forestry Commission, Areas of Outstanding Natural Beauty (AONB), Nature Reserves, Sites of Special Scientific Interest (SSSI), private estates and the MOD.

There are also No-Go zones within these designated areas. Some are purely seasonal, such as the nesting and shooting cycles on its grouse moors; or restrictions imposed by the farming practices of lambing and harvest. Others are of a more permanent nature as indicated by the omnipresent Red Flags surrounding the MOD camps of Otterburn and Redesdale.

Considerate walkers will appreciate that the great majority of walks in the guide are on waymarked public paths, bridleways, byways and permissive paths, with coastal walks utilising the permitted ground between low and high water marks. If in doubt please verify the route with an OS 1:25,000 map and / or the County Rights of Way Officer or the Pathway Officers of the designated bodies - see 'Useful Information'. The few sections of routes that are not shown as public pathways have been cleared after consultation with the appropriate landowner, ranger or warden.

Accommodation

The majority of walks have been selected, wherever possible, in clusters thus reducing the need for daily searches of overnight accommodation. Northumberland offers a wide range of overnight stays to suit all tastes, including eight youth hostels, several bunkhouses plus bothies, a wide range of campsites and caravan parks, in addition to country hotels, village inns and B&Bs. As the final stages of the Pennine Way pass through Northumberland it is advisable to book en-route accommodation in advance during the summer months; this includes the four hostels along the way.

Accommodation details can be obtained from the local Tourist Information Centres (listed in 'Useful Information'), who also offer an accommodation booking service.

GUIDE TO THE GUIDE

Aim

To produce a walks guide that enables the reader and the walker to enjoy the delights and surprises of Northumberland. A book that hopefully conveys the author's enthusiasm for this relatively unknown, but incomparably diverse and extensive county; a work that is as expressively spirited as it is literally stimulating and honest.

The 35 walks within the guide sample Northumberland's scenic strengths as found in its Cheviot hills, its crags and dales and coastline, providing a mix to suit pedestrians of all interests and abilities.

Layout

The guide contains three chapters, each covering a specific topography that is uniquely Northumbrian. Chapter 1 includes nine walks in the Cheviot Hills, England's most isolated range, the majority of which are, by the very nature of the terrain, for the upland enthusiast. Chapter 2 traverses Northumberland's crags and dales offering 18 stimulating scenic walks of character, never two the same. Chapter 3 embraces, in 8 walks, 48 miles of sweeping sands and dimpled dunes decorated by massive castles and pensive priories, a coastline that has no equal on England's shores. Finally, there are thumb-nail sketches of seven Long Distance Walks that enter into, or pass through, Northumberland.

Whatever your interests are when walking, they can be identified with a specific walk by means of the Special Interests Table that follows this section. A Glossary of Northumberland names and dialect words, with local pronunciations, is followed by the Bibliography and, finally, Useful Information.

Chapters 1 to 3

Each chapter of walks is introduced by a landscape portrait and a brief outline of the highlights of each walk. Each walk carries a fact file, detailing the **Type of Walk, Maps, Start/Finish, Distance, Height Gain, Grade, Walking Time, Accommodation & Parking,** with a simple sketch map showing the designated route. This is then followed by a detailed route description that includes prominent and permanent features together with grid references and compass bearings if necessary. The directive 'left/right' is invariably confirmed by the instruction 'i.e. east/west'. The whole is then completed with numbered 'Items of Interest Along the Way', each being keyed into the route description, e.g. Harthope Linn (1) or Bone Floor (2). The **Grade** is classified from 1 to 4, 1 being a short walk by distinct paths with few or no ascents; 4 is invariably in excess of 10 miles with steep or long ascents, requiring map and compass skills. **Walking Time** is calculated by using W.W. Naismith's established formula - 'for each 3 miles (4.8km) of linear distance allow 1 hour, and should height gain be achieved in that distance add 30 minutes for each 1000ft (305m) of ascent', tempered with my own experiences concerning terrain, weather conditions and convenience stops. The guide was written with pleasure and enjoyment in mind, and as such may ere on the slow side. Let each walker proceed with a whistle as they walk, for if you can't whistle you're walking too fast!

SPECIAL INTEREST TABLE

Interest	Chapter	Walk
ANTIQUITY	1	1, 2, 3, 6, 7, 8, 9
	2	10, 12, 13, 14, 15, 16
	3	
DROVE ROADS	1	2, 7, 8, 9
	2	13, 16, 17, 20, 24, 25, 27
	3	
ECCLESIASTICAL	1	1, 8, 9
	2	11, 12, 13, 15, 23, 24, 25, 27
	3	28, 30, 31, 32, 33, 34, 35
FLORA & FAUNA	1	1, 3, 5, 6, 7, 8, 9
	2	10, 11, 13, 14, 15, 16, 17, 20, 21, 22, 23, 24, 25, 26, 27
	3	28, 29, 30, 31, 32, 33, 34, 35
GEOLOGY	1	3, 4, 5, 6 7, 9
	2	11, 12, 13, 14, 15, 16, 20, 21, 24, 25, 26, 27
	3	30, 31, 32, 33, 34, 35
HISTORICAL	1	1, 2, 3, 6, 7, 8, 9
	2	10, 11, 12, 13, 14, 15, 16, 17, 20, 21, 22, 23, 24, 25, 27
	3	28, 29, 30, 31, 32, 33, 34, 35
LITERARY	1	4
	2	15, 16, 26, 27
	3	28, 29, 30, 31, 32
OLD INDUSTRY	1	6, 7, 9
	2	10, 11, 12, 13, 15, 16, 17, 21, 22, 23, 24, 25, 26, 27
	3	28, 29, 30, 31, 32, 33, 34, 35
PHOTOGRAPHY	1	1, 2, 3, 5, 6, 7, 8, 9
	2	10, 11, 12, 13, 14, 15, 16, 20, 21, 22, 23, 24, 25, 27
	3	28, 29, 30, 31, 32, 33, 34, 35
SCENIC BEAUTY	1	1, 2, 3, 4, 5 ,6, 7, 8, 9
	2	10, 11, 12, 13, 14, 15, 16, 17, 20, 22, 23, 24, 25, 27
	3	28, 29, 30, 31, 32, 33, 34, 35
WALKS - CHALLENGING	1	4, 5, 7, 8, 9
	2	11, 14, 15, 16, 25
	3	30

Interest	Chapter	Walk
WALKS - GENTLE	1	1
	2	17
	3	28, 29, 31
WATERCOURSES	1	1, 2, 4, 7, 9
	2	12, 15, 16, 17, 20, 21, 22, 23, 24, 25, 26, 27
	3	28, 29, 30, 35

CLOTHING and EQUIPMENT

What do I wear for a leisurely ramble along the golden sands of Beadnell Bay on a balmy summer's day, or for a high level trek to Cheviot's summit in winter's grip? Three words provide the answer - Conditions, Common Sense.

Conditions Overhead

Northumberland, although perched on the north-eastern corner of England, is not prone to the deluges experienced in the 'honey-pot' walking areas. Nor is it subjected to the howling Hebridean gales and Siberian cold met on many Munroes, for there is but one summit (plus one top) exceeding 2500ft (762m) and only four Donalds, i.e. 2000-2500ft (610m-762m) plus two tops. There are however rare occasions when they too experience winter's icy grip when a thin and fractious north-easter screams in over the North Sea, making the eyes water and testing the resolve of even the most hardy of hill walkers.

Therefore when winter winds threaten, the Wind Chill factor must always be considered - an increase of 10 miles per hour in wind speed can reduce the temperature from 18°C to 7°C, or in colder conditions from 10°C to -13°C. Bear in mind also the Lapse Rate - the higher the climb the lower the temperature, for every 1000ft ascended there is a reduction of approximately 3°C.

Temperature and moisture are of prime importance to the Northumbrian walker; if both are in agreeable symmetry then the journey will be a pleasure. If not, and the hiker is ill-prepared and ill-equipped, they run the twin risks of exposure to hypothermia or dehydration/heat exhaustion. Hypothermia can strike if the temperature of the body core drops below 98.4°F in continuous cold and wet conditions. Dehydration or heat exhaustion can be induced by exposing the body, and in particular the head, to excess sun's rays/heat coupled with an inadequate liquid intake.

Conditions Underfoot

The Cheviot Hills, Rothbury Forest, North Tynedale, South Tynedale, East and West Allen Dales at lower levels are traversed either by forest roads, farm tracks, miner's/carrier's ways or grass covered paths, and invariably provide good dry walking. At higher levels conditions vary, from dry pathways over springy grass, as on the summits of Hedgehope, Little Ward Law and The Dodd, to blankets of tousy tangled heather on Simonside and Rig Cairn, and mires or hags of seeping peat as encountered on the heights of Peel Fell and The Cheviot.

Vegetation invariably provides a reliable indicator as to what lies beneath. Avoid patches of bright green sphagnum or featherbed moss, both flourish in wet, watery conditions. Cotton grass and rush should also be avoided if possible. Bilberry, bents, molinia and matgrass however signal dry conditions underfoot.

Choose footwear that will be warm and dry in winter, cool and comfortable in summer. Footwear chosen wisely will lighten the step; take the wrong option and the walk could be a disaster.

Suggestions

Veteran and card-carrying pedestrians invariably include a proven talisman in the sack to ward off elemental spirits. It may only be a de-rigeur black bin liner to keep your cake dry, or a phial of Diethyltoluamide (repellent) to ward off the winged nasties found in forest or areas of water and on the heathery fells at dawn. May I also suggest the following which will enable the Northumberland walker to make a balanced choice.

High Level

Winter - A windproof and waterproof jacket/cagoule, waterproof overtrousers or gaiters, woolly hat, gloves/mitts and a survival bag. Also high energy food for a long trek and emergency rations, such as dried fruit, dark chocolate, fruit cake (if in season) plus a hot drink.

Summer - Lightweight clothing and protective hat, with a windproof/waterproof jacket in the sack, plus a large water filled bottle.

Low Level

Summer - In hot sunny conditions, for Northumberland receives more than the national average in sheltered valleys or on exposed coasts, the walker if unprotected can suffer from dehydration/heat exhaustion. A lightweight, broad-brimmed cotton hat and a plentiful supply of water will provide all the protection needed, coupled with a proprietary suncream for the prevention of sunburn on exposed parts. The contentious issue of shorts versus lightweight trousers is a matter, I would suggest, of personal preference and individual choice.

SAFETY

Safety in the great outdoors is something we must all be aware of. A careless or unguarded step could break a bone or tear a tendon, causing a problem for the walker, and if journeying alone, a major problem. High level fell walks in Northumberland are more often than not completed in total solitude; it is therefore essential to possess a basic knowledge of emergency procedures and the equipment needed to minimise discomfort and aid rescue.

Equipment

1) First Aid Kit, including sterile dressings, zinc tape, antiseptic cream, crepe/elasticated bandages (tubi-grip), scissors/knife and medication. *The medication is for personal use only; do not administer medication to another unless medically qualified.*

2) A basic knowledge of First Aid should be carried in the head or in the sack.

3) A knife, torch (with spare bulb and batteries), whistle, spare laces (double up as binding), emergency food and drinking water, survival bag, compass, map, paper and pen/pencil.

Action

Risks can be reduced by observing a few simple guidelines and using that most under employed asset - common sense.

1) Prevention is always better than cure, as advocated by the Victorian mountaineer Edward Whymper - 'heed well the placement of your feet'.

2) Solitude in the hills is much sought after, but with regard to safety should be avoided or insured against by informing someone of your route and estimated time of return (ETR). Alternatively, leave your route plan with details of destination, colour of garments and the ETR in a visible position in your car, if travelling by car. Such an action is thought by some to be an open invitation to the car thief, but consider, cars and their accessories can be replaced when lost, human life cannot.

3) Should you be immobilised and require help, use the International Rescue Call - *six long blasts on a whistle, or flashes with a torch, repeated at one minute intervals; the acknowledging reply - three short blasts at one minute intervals.* Should you be without whistle or torch SHOUT using the same code. Whilst waiting for help utilise the terrain to gain protection from the elements by sheltering on the lee-side of outcrops, hags, walls etc. from wind and rain/snow, or the sun in summer. Use spare clothing/survival bag, with feet pointing to the wind to maintain body temperature.

4) If with companions fix your position - a six figure grid reference - onto paper; Eastings first, i.e. the immediate vertical grid line to the left of your position, then the number of tenths from the grid line to your position, then Northings - repeat the procedure using the horizontal grid line below the position, as instructed on the legend of the OS map. Also put to paper the name and age of the injured person, injury and time sustained, general health, clothing including colour, and dispatch an able-bodied companion to the nearest telephone (public telephone as per OS map or farmhouse). Dial 999 (police) who will alert and co-ordinate the local Search and Rescue Team. When a Search and Rescue Team is requested, the casualty MUST STAY PUT until help arrives.

Harthope Linn (Walk 4)

Crossing Kelpie Strand to Hedgehope (Walk 5)
Into Alwin Valley (Walk 8)

MAPS LEGEND

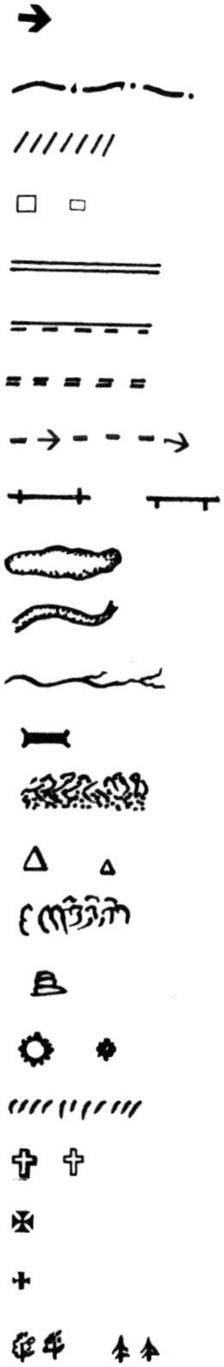

START OF WALK

BOUNDARY - NATIONAL/COUNTY

VILLAGE/TOWNSHIP

FARM BUILDING/HOUSE

CLASSIFIED ROAD

UNCLASSIFIED ROAD

FARM, FOREST OR CART TRACK

ROUTE/FOOTPATH WITH DIRECTION

RAILWAY - IN USE/DISUSED

LAKE/RESERVOIR

RIVER/WATER

BURN/STREAM

BRIDGE

CLIFFS

MOUNTAIN/HILL SUMMIT

CRAG/CLIFF

CAIRN

PREHISTORIC FORT/SETTLEMENT

CULTIVATION TERRACES

ABBEY, PRIORY OR CHURCH

CASTLE

PELE TOWER/BASTLE

FOREST/WOOD (BROAD LEAFED/CONIFERS)

CHAPTER 1
The Cheviot Hills

Hills of sheep, and the homes of silent vanquished races,
And winds, austere and pure.
R.L. Stevenson

How apt and pure the words of Robert Louis Stevenson, when applied to the flowing domes and rippling ridges of the Cheviot Hills, Northumberland's silent Border bastions and England's northern marches. Lonely hills of granite and moors of fading windswept grass and bible-black heather, they range eastward from Peel Fell to the valley of the Till. Although the Cheviots straddle the Border Line, most of the range resides in Northumberland and includes the massif of The Cheviot and its outlyers. Hills and mountains that provide endless solitudinous miles of unique upland form, where the turmoil of the past has softened and mellowed, as has the landscape, to provide some of the finest wilderness walking in England. Certainly without doubt the most secluded, with little but the wuthering wind and the wistful cries of moorland birds for company; where even the occasional stands of ubiquitous conifer have failed to change the Cheviot's face.

Perhaps as mountain ranges go the Cheviots are not eye-catching or spectacularly high like some of the overcrowded mountain playgrounds, though they do include five mountains above 2000ft (610m) - The Cheviot, Hedgehope Hill, Cushat Law, Bloodybush Edge and Windy Gyle - with Muckle Cheviot topping them all at 2676ft (815m); plus three tops above 2000ft (610m) - Cairn Hill, Auchope Cairn and Comb Fell. Statistics that may suggest, along with distant fleeting glances, that the Cheviots are a characterless upland plateau with few distinguishing landmarks.

On-foot acquaintance immediately dispels such misconceptions, for springing from the writhing ridges and domed summits of the Cheviot range are rushing, tumbling burns and rivers surging through a network of deep clefts and cleughs that, when seen from above, dispel any doubts of scenic dullness and upland boredom. For each cleugh or valley, gouged by the burns of Alwin, College, Harthope, Rowhope and Usway, plus the rivers Breamish and perhaps the finest of all the Coquet, is in its own subtle way a masterpiece of Cheviot sculpture that has few equals. Such deep and definite divides have created a network of high level, far seeing scenic ridges, which when crowned with grassy waymarked ways provide endless passage that has few equals in England's uplands.

THE WALKS

Nine rewarding walks in the Cheviot Hills have been selected, varying from a 5 mile stroll above the tree-lined banks of the winsome College Burn, to a high level trek of 16 miles encircling the lonely heights of Breamish. **Walk 1** provides a gentle introduction to the foothills of the Cheviot and its high interest circuit of the lower reaches of the College Burn, with **Walk 2** venturing that little bit further and higher from the same valley to prehistoric sites and England's border, with far reaching views into the Tweed Valley. Remaining with the eastern hills **Walk 3** rises for a bird's-eye view of Milfield Plain and Ice Age channels, leading into the whitelands wilderness below the Cheviot massif. **Walk 4** is a challenging walk to Muckle Cheviot's summit, with great rewards for the prepared enthusiast; and for those who prefer the direct route to a mountain's summit **Walk 5**'s ascent of neighbouring Hedgehope Hill provides just that. **Walk 6** visits the intriguing Breamish Valley, south of Hedgehope, for a journey into the Bronze and Iron Ages; with **Walk 7** stretching legs and lungs for a high level scenic circuit of the lower, middle and upper Breamish Valley. **Walks 8 and 9** venture into upper Coquet Dale, Northumberland's finest trout river, for their circular walks. Walk 8 follows the jinking Alwin Valley to fringe Cushat Law and Bloodybush Edge, returning by the scenic route of the old drove road of Clennell Street, while Walk 9 is a joyous hike, by grassy ridgeways to the Border's grandstand of Windy Gyle, returning to the tinkling Coquet by 'The Clattering Path'.

Walk 1: The Old Ways

HETHPOOL, OLD YEAVERING & COLLEGE BURN

Type of Walk: *A tempting taste of the fell fringes of the Cheviot Hills is offered in this distinctive and frequently waymarked circular walk by way of public and permissive paths. The walk provides an ideal introduction to Northumberland's hill country, offering fine views, a historic past and wildlife galore, although some sections can be wet underfoot after periods of precipitation.*

Maps: OS 1:25 000 Outdoor Leisure 16, The Cheviot Hills
OS 1:50 000 Landranger Sheet 75, Berwick-upon-Tweed

Start/Finish: Hethpool - GR 895283, on a branch road from the B6351. 1½ miles (2.4km) S from Kirknewton, 8 miles (12.8km) W from Wooler by the B6351.

Distance: 5½ miles (8.8km)

Height Gain: 394ft (120m)

Grade: 2

Walking Time: 2½-3 hours

Accommodation & Parking:
Accommodation, including a youth hostel, available in Wooler. Car park S of Hethpool cottages.

John highte that oon and Allyn that oother;
Of o toon they born that highte strother
Far in the north I can nat tell where,
Chaucer, *The Reeve's Tale*

The Route: Walk north beyond the car park conifers, cross the cattle grid to Hethpool cottages and Hethpool Manor (1). At the fingerpost 'Old Yeavering 2½ miles' turn right onto a farm track leading to a bridge spanning the peat-stained waters of the gurgling College Burn (2). Once over swing left, at the waymark, to rise with the stony track into a gated plantation.

The wet ride through the spruce is left by sturdy stile, in favour of a narrow trod north-east over a stone-strewn pasture. The Cheviots are now upon us, dominating our immediate right with the overpowering bulk of Newton Tors, crowned with the cairned and craggy summits of Hare Law, Wester Tor and Easter Tor. To the north beyond the tree-lined College Burn stands The Bell, its west

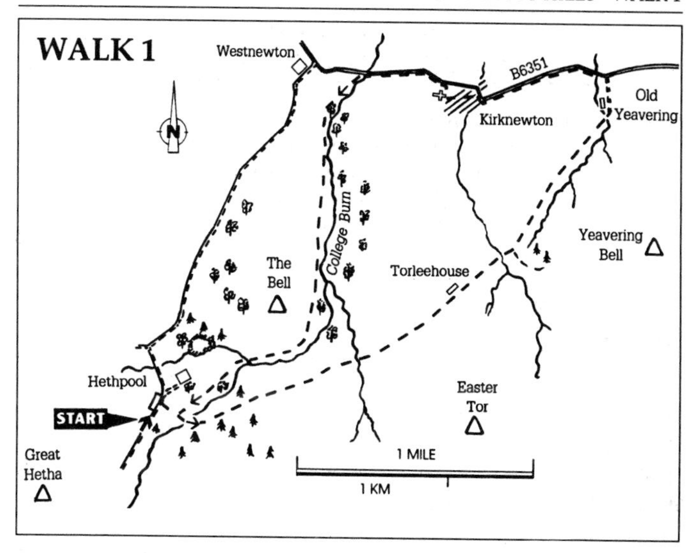

flank oak-cloaked by Hethpoolbell Wood (3) and its southern aspect a scatter of scree and colourful gorse. Ahead, the stiled rise breaches a narrow, gorse-filled gully crossing a second rock and 'thorn scattered pasture to a square sheep stell, before joining a rutted cart track north-east to Torleehouse (4). At 590ft (180m) this is the highest point of the outward journey, providing appealing views of the fortified summit of Yeavering Bell's classic cone (5). The view to the right now reveals the flat and fertile acres of Milfield Plain, framed to the east by the bastion of Doddington Moor.

The steady descent into the Glen valley, alongside the cleft of Yeavering Burn, on a fine wide track to Old Yeavering (6) is a delight, passing two cottages prior to linking with the B6351. Swing left onto this country lane for a brisk half-mile hike, along the meagre verge, to the clustered dwellings and church of Kirknewton (7).

Continue west with the B6351 past the old railway station and station master's house, to cross the College Burn via the three-arched stone bridge. At the finger post, 'Hethpool $1^{3}/_{4}$ miles', turn sharp left to begin the pleasing return alongside and above the western banks of the College. A way, rich in birdlife and colourfully strewn with flowers and scrub, best seen in April-May in the glad times of spring when the entire valley is aflame with the yellows of whin.

The waymarked path, although narrow and twisting, winds south with the burn, first by bankside then over a high bluff for 1/2 mile (0.8km). *This waymarked public path is at variance with the OS Map Outdoor Leisure 16 - The Cheviot Hills, which shows a public path south and east of the river.* At the whin-bound haughs rise right, by gate and stile, to reach the high side of an established strip of venerable oaks. Continue south between the bracken-clad flank of The Bell and the plantation fence, and where the scree encroaches from the right draw close to the fence, crossing it by waymarked stile onto a descending path through bracken and thorn.

Further stiles assist passage as the now booming, but unseen, College Burn is approached. Fortunately a honeysuckle bedecked footbridge is at hand to reveal its picturesque progress through rocky defiles to the tumbling white water of Hethpool Linn. *Keep to the paths and the footbridge* before returning west, for the final 1/2 mile (0.8km), through the waymarked haughs below Hethpool Manor to the outward track, Hethpool cottages and the car park.

ITEMS OF INTEREST ALONG THE WAY

(1) HETHPOOL MANOR. Circa 1919, on the site of the seventeenth century manor. The present house adjoins the ruins of an early fifteenth century pele tower, which was mentioned in the mid 1500s as 'a lytle stone house that is a greate releyffe to the tennents', i.e. from the attentions of the plundering Scots reivers.

(2) COLLEGE BURN. Its Anglo-Saxon name indicates, not a seat of learning, but 'a stream in the wet land'. Originating from Cheviot's seeping hags, this most intriguing burn flows rapidly through the Hen Hole to the scoured wetlands of the College valley.

(3) HETHPOOLBELL WOOD. Centuries ago oak graced the Cheviot Hills, sadly few remain today. Hethpoolbell Wood is an exception, thanks to the foresight of Admiral Lord Collingwood, second in command to Admiral Lord Nelson. Resident at Hethpool Manor, so keen was he to ensure a constant supply of timber for the navy's needs he always carried a pouch of acorns and in 1828 stated, 'I plant

College Valley from Westnewton Bridge

an oak wherever I have a place to put it in'.

(4) TORLEEHOUSE. This isolated shieling was originally known as Tarleazes, Anglo-Saxon, meaning a clearing on the hill. Today it serves as a well kept riding stable.

(5) YEAVERING BELL. Standing north from the Cheviot outlyers this conical hill is capped by the largest prehistoric fort in Northumberland. Its embankments and surrounding ditches are of prominent proportions and the views from its summit all embracing.

(6) OLD YEAVERING. Probably the site of the sixth century Anglian timber palace of the Northumbrian kings, a building unique in Britain, referred to by St Bede as 'Ad Gefrin'. Nearby, in the River Glen, the early Christian St Paulinus allegedly baptised thousands of Northumbrians in the space of 36 days.

(7) KIRKNEWTON. A peaceful, typically Northumbrian, hamlet said to be the one mentioned in the introductory lines by Chaucer. The church, with pieces of the original twelfth century construction remaining, displays a simple relief on the east wall of the nave illustrating the 'Adoration of the Magi', and clothed in the dress of the time - the Kilt.

Walk 2: Northumberland's Alpine Valley
HETHPOOL, ECCLES CAIRN and the COLLEGE VALLEY

Type of Walk: *A stimulating walk, seen at its best on a clear spring day when the larks are high above the fells and the secluded alpine College Valley is a blaze of yellow whin. By waymarked lanes, upland pasture paths and plantation tracks this walk provides an abundance of wildlife on the scenic close-ups of Newton Tors and Cheviot.*

Maps: OS 1:25 000 Outdoor Leisure 16, The Cheviot Hills
OS 1:50 000 Landranger Sheet 74, Kelso & surrounding area

Start/Finish: Hethpool in the College Valley, GR 895283, 2 miles (3.2km) SSW on a minor road from Westnewton on the B6351

Distance: 8 miles (12.8km)

Height Gain: 1024ft (312m)

Grade: 3

Walking Time: 4 hours

Accommodation & Parking:
A choice in Wooler; Kirk Yetholm - inn, B/Bs, Milfield - village B/Bs. Parking at Hethpool Estate's car park, GR 894281, 300yds/m SSW from Hethpool. Access beyond this point is by permit from Sale & Partners, Estate Office, Glendale Road, Wooler.

The Route: From Hethpool Estate's car park, with its information board and map welcoming valley walkers, turn right over the cattle-grid. Walk under the gaze of Newton Tors to the cottages and manor entrance of Hethpool (1), prior to veering left with the lane for a further 300yds/m to a gated junction. Bear left at the gate, marked 'St Cuthbert's Way, Trowupburn and Elsdonburn' onto a tarmac strip west. Immediately right the stepped *Cultivation Terraces* marked on the map are clearly visible, as the $1^{1}/_{2}$ mile (2.4km) lane winds south-west below Little Hetha. Fork west with Elsdon Burn, by the conifers to Elsdonburn Farm, into the isolated heart of Cheviot's foothills; hills that from prehistoric to medieval times succoured many.

Elsdonburn Farm buildings, signposted 'To the Border Ridge

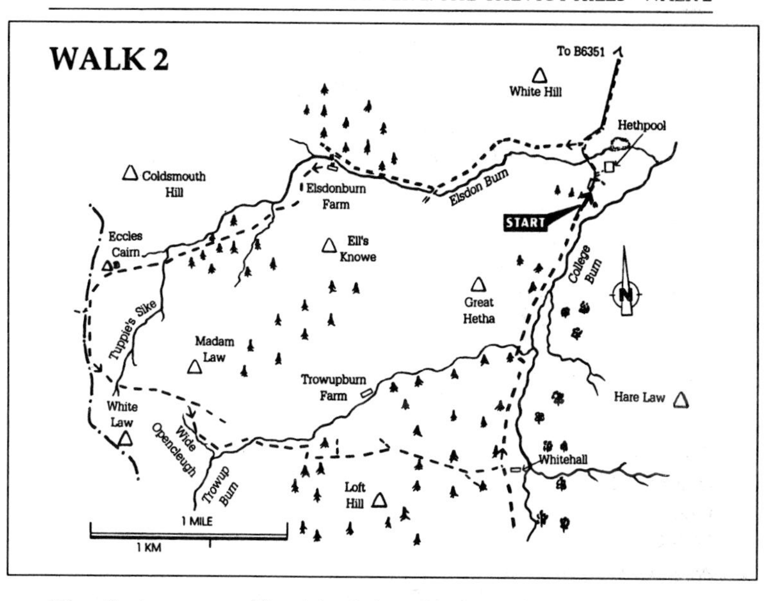

$1^{1}/_{2}$ miles', are passed by rising left and right with the gated pasture track running south-west above the gully of Elsdon Burn. Beyond the second gate fork right to cross Shank's Sike prior to crossing the pasture of Scaldhill Shank (a bearing of 251° magnetic) to the two-step stile and waymarked perimeter of Scaldhill plantation. Initially the narrow coniferous way runs through a pitch-black tunnel, before emerging by stile onto the fell. *This route through the conifers is not shown on the OS 1:50 000 Landranger 74 map.*

Ahead the grassy flanks of Eccles Cairn, its summit barely visible, can be seen rising beyond the damp surrounds of Tuppie's Sike (we pass its source later). Cross grassland and sike, (bearing 257° magnetic) by a series of waymarks to Eccles Cairn (2), a humped vantage point, although just off the public path, that provides breathtaking views of Tweeddale and the Borders. Leave this grandstand via a marked trod south-west to the Border Line. Do not follow the St Cuthberts Way into Scotland but walk south with the wall to gated White Swire (3).

Enjoy the view and listen to the past as well as the constant birdsong before leaving this historic gateway and its modern Pennine Way signpost. Follow the fine grass path running south-east and east, crossing the wet source of Tuppie's Sike by Maddie's Well and contouring the northern slopes of White Law to the gated col of Wideopen Head, below Madam Law.

Here Wide Opencleugh leads by thin trod into the glaciated valley of Trowup Burn below the sombre side of Shorthope Shank. Sheep stells and pens abound as the path veers left to cross a stiled wall then hops over the burn, which is followed east to a conglomeration of wood, metal and stone sheep pens. At the stone enclosure veer right alongside its wall, passing through a field gate, and right again through a wicket gate into a coniferous plantation east of Shorthope Burn.

Rise south between forest fence and perimeter trees to reach a rough forest road; cross and with the public footpath pass through the conifers east, emerging by stepped stile onto the rolling slopes of Loft Hill. Continue east with the waymarked path to the plantation ahead, no doubt admiring views of Trowupburn's white walled farm below, framed in the north-eastern quadrant by the profiles of Madam Law, Ell's Knowe and Great Hetha. A marked gate opens onto forest track descending east, with spectacular views of the College valley and Hare Law, as the narrow lane is met by Whitehall. Swing left onto the lane for a quiet scenic stroll north, of 1½ miles (2.4km) through this, Northumberland's most pleasing valley. To the right, over the whin-clad sweeps of College Burn (4), with the lower slopes of Hare Law and Wester Tor clad in the timber of Cheviot's old forests (5), we are funnelled towards the backdrop of The Bell beyond the car park and Hethpool.

ITEMS OF INTEREST ALONG THE WAY

(1) HETHPOOL. The 'Pool under Great Hetha', a nearby hill capped by the remains of a massive Iron Age fort. The present manor house stands by the ruins of a fourteenth century border pele tower; a protection against border reivers who poured over the border at White Swire.

(2) ECCLES CAIRN. Its summit the, now pillaged, burial chamber of an Iron Age chieftain. Cairns and atmospheric burial cists are also present on many surrounding heights, in particular the higher

College Valley north to The Bell

nearby summit of Coldsmouth Hill.

(3) WHITE SWIRE. Recorded as 'White Swyre' in AD 1222 when the Sheriff of Northumberland was ordered 'to travel to White Swyre, and there settle the Marches' (Border). A place of passage much used by reivers from both sides of the border, and later by local drovers.

(4) COLLEGE BURN. The name College is said to be taken from the Anglo-Saxon 'Cool-Leche' meaning a burn running through flat ground.

(5) ANCIENT WOODLANDS. In 1995 Hethpool Estates planted 70 hectares of native broadleaves to recreate the valley tree cover of old. Cover that in prehistoric times was present even on the summit of Cheviot.

Walk 3: Meltwater Channels and Bloody Remains
HUMBLETON HILL, TOM TALLON'S CRAG & COMMONBURN

Type of Walk: *Rising above Milfield Plain, the heights and meltwater channels of Humbleton and Harehope lead to a high plateau (clear day), traversing above Common Burn. An ideal walk for the inquisitive and energetic, with waymarked ways revealing a basket of summits and crags. Abundant moorland wildlife, historical remains and folklore complete the enjoyment.*

Maps: OS 1:25 000 Outdoor Leisure 16, The Cheviot Hills
OS 1:50 000 Landranger Sheet 75, Berwick-upon-Tweed

Start/Finish: Humbleton Burn, Forest Enterprise car park and nature trail, GR 976272. 1¼ miles (2km) WSW from Wooler market place, signposted 'FE Wooler Common', and 'St Cuthbert's Way'.

Distance: 8¾ miles (14km). A shorter walk of 3¼ miles (5.2km) is available

Height Gain: 1063ft (324m)

Grade: 3, in severe weather/poor visibility - 4

Walking Time: 4½-5 hours

Accommodation & Parking:
A range from hotels to youth hostel available in Wooler. Park at Humbleton Burn car park (free), GR 976272.

The Route: From the car park walk north beyond the information board, crossing Humbleton Burn onto the fenced Nature Trail. After approximately 100yds/m a grass footpath left, marked 'St Cuthbert's Way', ascends between larch and Douglas fir to a perimeter wall, seats and picnic bench. Pass through the wicket gate onto a bridleway twisting west, between a series of bracken clad glacial mounds north-east of Brown's Law. At the gated crosstracks, by sheep pens and an incongruous 'British Rail' wagon, pass through to turn right descending with a line of ageing ash to the red pantiles of High Humbleton (1). Immediately left the great bulk of Humbleton Hill (2) rears above, whilst ahead the flat fertile acres of Milfield Plain (3) lead the gaze north-east over the moors of Weetwood and Doddington (sites of Bronze Age 'cup and ring

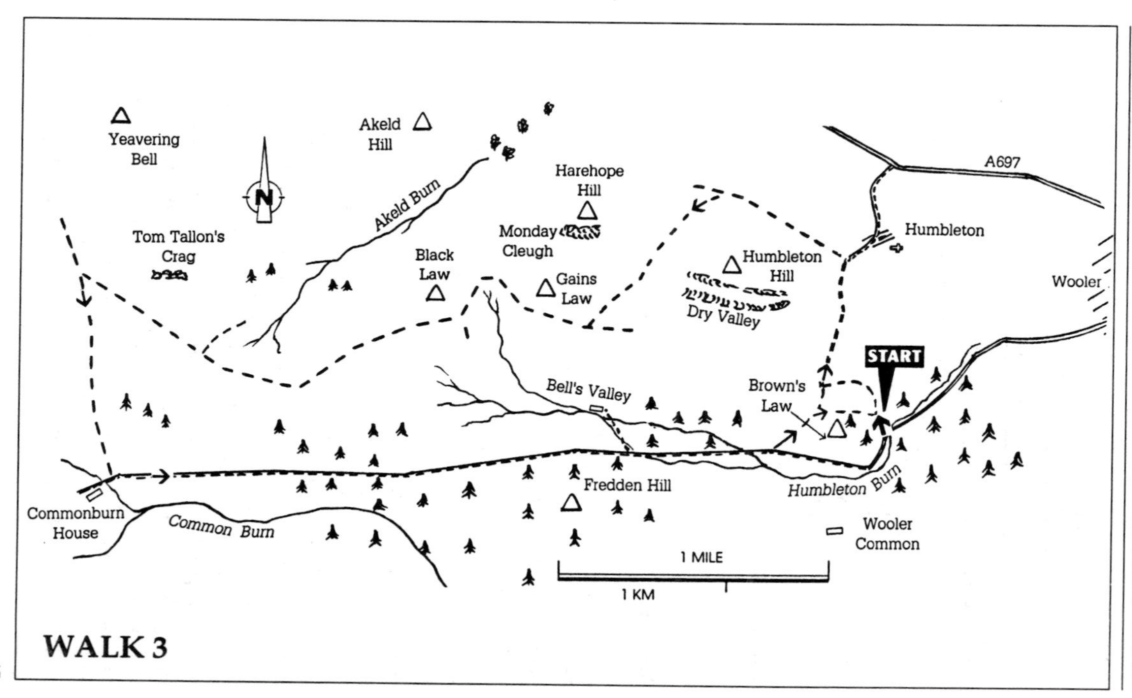
Yeavering Bell
Akeld Hill
Harehope Hill
A697
Humbleton
Akeld Burn
Tom Tallon's Crag
Black Law
Monday Cleugh
Gains Law
Humbleton Hill
Dry Valley
Wooler
START
Brown's Law
Bell's Valley
Fredden Hill
Humbleton Burn
Commonburn House
Common Burn
Wooler Common
1 MILE
1 KM
WALK 3

marks').

Prior to High Humbleton, a finger post, 'Cleadscleugh 1$^{1}/_{2}$ miles', directs us left, i.e. west-north-west on a gated cart track below the rock strewn upper slopes of Humbleton Hill. Don't let the views over the Milfield Plain prevent you from taking the left fork at a dual waymarked post, leaving the bridleway for an ascending footpath south-west between Humbleton and Harehope. The footpath is, in fact, a wide and initially rocky track ascending to the col between the two meltwater scarred hills. North, the rock and scree face of Monday Cleugh divides Harehope and Gains Law, whilst to the south the dry valley - Meltwater Channel (4) - slices through the skirts of Humbleton Hill. Footpath markers continue to guide the walker to the path junction below the summit bump of Gains Law.

Those wishing a short walk should turn left at the junction, returning below Cloudberry Hill to the outward path by Brown's Law. For the complete circuit turn right to pass Gains Law for a westerly 2$^{1}/_{2}$ mile (4km) scenic hike to below Tom Tallon's Crag, that provides a unique taste of the total isolation of the Cheviots. The route is waymarked and good underfoot, with a couple of exceptions: a) after leaving the wall west of Black Hill and b) west and below Tom Tallon's Crag; and take care once over the step-stiled fence at the cleugh head between Gains Law and Black Law to leave the fence right, 25yds/m over the stile, onto a narrow trod through heather. A map is essential on this section, not so much for navigation but to identify the dozens of surrounding hills, crags and cleughs.

The dolerite outcrop known as Tom Tallon's Crag (5) can be seen on the immediate skyline, north of the public path which leads north-west through heather and tussock to a prominent dual marker post and cairn at GR 928282. A path that focuses attention, not on the crag but on the great prehistoric walled fort astride the twin domes of Yeavering Bell (6). Turn sharp left at the marked and cairned junction, to begin the trek south to Commonburn House Farm, veering left at the first fork to descend straight to the valley and farm of Common Burn. The aspect ahead is highlighted by a crescent of Cheviot's outlyers, curving east over Great Moor and Preston Hill to Broadhope Hill, Hawsen Crags and Cold Law.

The final 3¼ miles (5.2km) is alongside, or on the central grass strip of Commonburn Lane. A straight untrammelled way that provides nothing but ever freshening views with grouse, peewit, lark, weasel, rabbit and hare for company, as it skirts the coniferous flank of Fredden Hill to meet the gorse-clad shoulders of Coldberry Hill and Brown's Law. Here we leave the lane left for a waymarked grassy ascent of Brown's Law, and a bracken lined descent to the ladder stile into the larch of our outward path from the car park. If time and energy allow why not explore the adjoining Nature Trail.

ITEMS OF INTEREST ALONG THE WAY

(1) HIGH HUMBLETON. Today a tiny hamlet, but in 1296 it was taxed at £39 per annum under the Lay Subsidy Rules, later developing into a cluster of cottages and a church with consecrated ground around a village green.

(2) HUMBLETON HILL. A hill topped with the remains of a Bronze and Iron Age fort and associated enclosures. Practically every summit on this eastern perimeter of the Cheviots carried a fort or encampment, with still visible hut circles, curricks and settlements. When the Romans arrived they took over many of these encampments, which in turn were re-occupied by the local tribes when the Romans retreated.

(3) MILFIELD PLAIN. As aerial views suggest the plain was once covered by a shallow lake. Climatic changes and drainage skills produced the fertile farmland we see today.

(4) MELTWATER CHANNELS. Monday Cleugh and the deep cleft riven in the south side of Humbleton Hill were channelled by meltwater, under pressure, beneath the ice cap during the last Ice Age. They and the surrounding mounds of glacial debris, indicate the directional flow, north-west to south-east, of the ice. It is said that in the vicinity of Monday Cleugh, the battle of 'Homildon' between Northumbrians and Scots resulted in bloodshed and great slaughter. Indeed a field at lower level, marked by a great standing stone, has yielded a crop of human skulls and horse bones.

(5) TOM TALLON'S CRAG. In folklore often referred to as Tom Tallon's grave, on account of a burial cist being discovered close to rocky outcrops. The name is derived from the Celtic words 'tomen' - a promontory, and 'llan' - enclosure.

(6) YEAVERING BELL. On its summit, ringed by the remains of a circlet of stones, stands the largest Iron Age fort in Northumberland. Within the outer wall earthworks and ditches, together with the foundations of horseshoe dwellings with the open side facing south, can be observed.

Walk 4: Muckle Cheviot

HARTHOPE BURN, CAIRN HILL, CHEVIOT AND SCALD HILL

Type of Walk: *In summer, with the singing larks, this ascent over the whale-back of Cheviot is a pleasing hike of interest, splendid views and much satisfaction. Beneath a howling winter's gale, smothered in clag, it is a serious undertaking, never to be underestimated. Navigation, thanks to public footpaths, waymarked permissive paths, slabbed ways, guiding fences and burnside paths, save for the short ascent to Cairn Hill, presents no problems. I can best summarise the walk with 'know your mountain, know yourself and be prepared'.*

Maps: OS 1:25 000 Outdoor Leisure 16, The Cheviot Hills
OS 1:25 000 Pathfinder, Sheet NT 82/92
OS 1:50 000 Landranger, Sheets 74 (Kelso) & 80 (The Cheviot Hills)

Start/Finish: In signposted upper Harthope valley,. by the small roadbridge, GR 953225, NE of Langleeford Farm; 5 miles (8km) SW from Wooler.

Distance: 8$^{1}/_{2}$ miles (13.6km)

Height Gain: 2028ft (618m)

Grade: 4

Walking Time: 5$^{1}/_{2}$ hours

Accommodation & Parking:
Wooler provides a range of accommodation, from hotels to youth hostel. Specified parking on the grass verges $^{1}/_{2}$ mile (0.8km) NE of Langleeford.

The forest of Chevyotte ys a mounteyne or greatt hyll, four myles or more of lengthe, and towards the northe it devydeth England and Scotland by the heighte of yt, as the water descendeth and

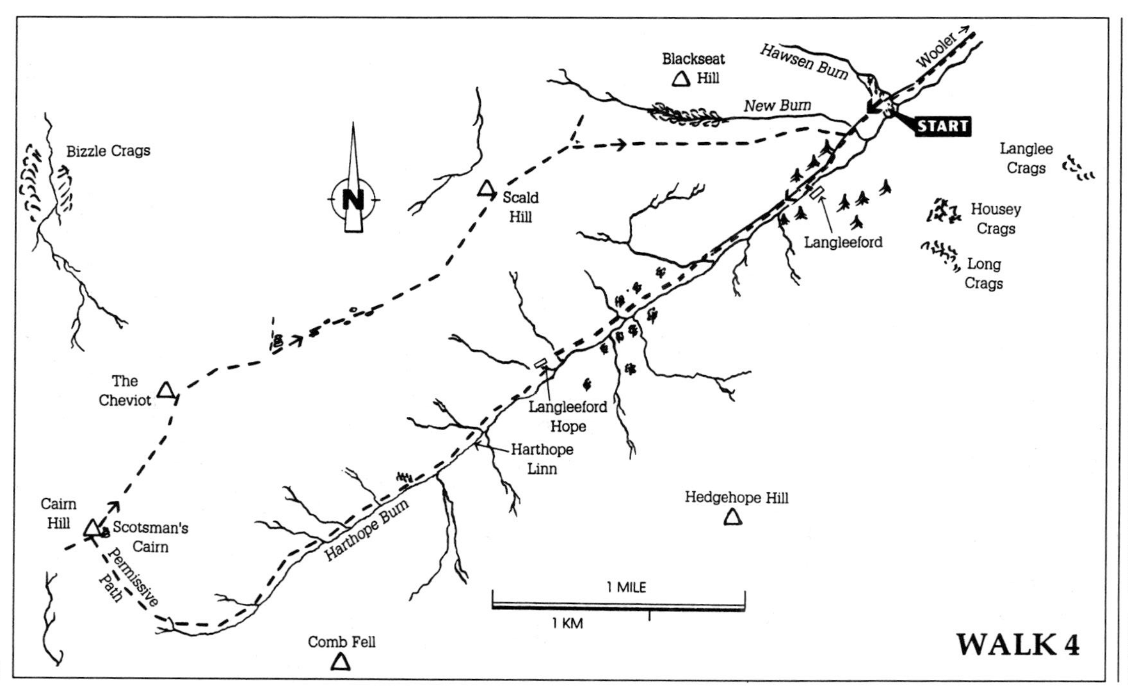
WALK 4
Wooler
START
Hawsen Burn
Blackseat Hill
New Burn
Langlee Crags
Housey Crags
Long Crags
Langleeford
Bizzle Crags
N
Scald Hill
The Cheviot
Langleeford Hope
Harthope Linn
Cairn Hill
Scotsman's Cairn
Permissive Path
Harthope Burn
Hedgehope Hill
1 MILE
1 KM
Comb Fell

falleth. And the most parte thereof, and especially towarde the heighte, ys a wete flowe mosse, so depe that scarcely eyther horse or cattal may go thereupon

Survey of the Waste Lands, 1542

Little has changed, save Cheviot in its entirety is now in England.

The Route: By exploring the picturesque upper reaches of Harthope valley (1) and then ascending to Cairn Hill, we are not tackling Cheviot's summit direct, thus avoiding the immediate tedium of Scald Hill and a steep ascent to the summit plateau.

Walk south-west on the tarmac lane, noting the finger post 'Scald Hill & Cheviot' - our return route, prior to passing by the half-hidden whitewashed buildings of Langleeford (2). Continue south-west by farm track, stiles and fords for the next 1¼ miles (2km) to skirt Langleeford Hope farm, north and south, by waymarked path; a section of nature's noises, in whose lower reaches oak, ash, alder and other rammell woods (3) grow.

With the last habitation now behind us the way is alongside the burn via ever shrinking grass paths/trods, as we first hear, then see the shy, pencil-thin cascade of Harthope Linn (1). Approach the waterfall's steep and unstable banks with caution. As the valley narrows between the steep flanks of Cheviot, Hedgehope and Comb Fell both burn and trod wind below clutches of diminutive alder, mountain ash and silver birch, clinging to the rocky banks. Look out for busy dippers, elusive ring ouzels and primroses as the tinkling waters hurry over a series of cascading linns.

1½ miles (2.4km) beyond the linn, at a point where the infant burn runs below a gully of naked earth, cross a small feeder as the public footpath peters out at GR 907191. Swing right from the burnside, bearing 324° magnetic, climbing quite sharply over matgrass and heather on the faint permissive path for 550yds (0.5km), to the stone pile, Scotsman's Cairn, topping Cairn Hill.

Cross by stile onto the slabs of the Pennine Way, north-east to the ailing, indeed sinking, triangulation pillar, over endless peat hags, black as sin and just as easy to fall into, capping Cheviot's summit plateau (4). As the flat summit reveals little but darkened desolation, carry on north-east with the permissive path to Scald Hill; initially parallel to the right hand fence, heading for a teetering guide post and the shelter cairn astride the 800m contour.

Descent from Cheviot begins from this cairn, a scenic route, assisted first by thirteen small marker-cairns, then steeply by an exposed and eroded wound in Cheviot's peaty shoulder, to level out with the fence line over a miry saddle leading to Scald Hill. Its summit is accessed by stile, then from here, with great views of the surrounding crags, by guiding fence north-east then east for the final descent, over a sea of heather, to the valley floor. Exit by the finger post noted at the start of our outward journey.

ITEMS OF INTEREST ALONG THE WAY

(1) HARTHOPE VALLEY, BURN & LINN. An ice-fashioned, geological fault between Hedgehope Hill and Cheviot; narrow, isolated and picturesque. The burn springs to life on the upper slopes of Cheviot's Cairn Hill. Its largest waterfall, Harthope Linn, plunges 25ft through a narrow defile.

(2) LANGLEEFORD. Alongside Harthope Burn, with a pedigree dating back to the sixteenth century when night sentries were posted to warn of Border reivers rampaging down the Harthope from Scotsman's Knowe (Cairn). In more peaceful times, c1791, a young Sir Walter Scott spent a happy holiday at Langleeford, recording 'Behold a letter from the mountains, for I am snugly settled here in the centre of the Cheviot Hills, in one of the wildest and most romantic situations'.

(3) RAMMELL WOOD. As mentioned in the *Survey of the Waste Lands* 1542, is natural regenerated coppiced wood.

(4) THE CHEVIOT 2676ft (815m). Pronounced 'Chee-veot', known locally as 'Muckle Cheviot' or simply 'Cheviot'. Northumberland's highest, best known, though not best loved, mountain is of volcanic origins. A mass of impervious granite and igneous rocks, rounded by time, weather and the abrasions of ice. Its surface, once tree covered, is now wrapped in glutinous heather-capped peat, with rock only revealed, in quantity, within the clefts of the Hen Hole and The Bizzle.

Stories about Cheviot abound, from trembling Daniel Defoe, who quaked in his saddle whilst ascending Cheviot shrieking 'he was much afraid of a knife edged ridge'! to Sheila, the Border Collie, awarded the Dicken Medal for her endeavours in the search and rescue of the crew of a B17 Flying-Fortress, crashed near Braydon Crag in the winter of 1944. Twisted remains emerge and submerge depending on the water content of the peat.

Walk 5: Northumberland's Olympus
HARTHOPE VALLEY & HEDGEHOPE HILL

Type of Walk: *A return linear, encompassing the wild and lonely lands that grace the roof of Northumberland. The ascent of 1640ft (500m) to Hedgehope's summit, on waymarked permissive tracks and trods, is in the main unremitting, over a mixture of upland terrain which can be wet in places. The rewards however are high and best appreciated on a clear day.*

The route or sections of the route taken by Permissive Paths may, unlike designated Rights of Way, be changed from time to time. In the event of any such changes to the Permissive Paths within Northumberland National Park, up-to-date details of the alterations will be displayed, together with strategically sited waymarks en route.

Maps: OS 1:25 000 Outdoor Leisure 16, The Cheviot Hills

OS 1:50 000 Landranger Sheets 74 (Kelso) & 80 (The Cheviot Hills)

Start/Finish: GR 953225, NE of Langleeford Farm in upper Harthope valley, 5 miles (8km) SW of Wooler. Northumberland National Park maps/path details on display.

Distance: 5 1/4 miles (8.4km)

Height Gain: 1640ft (500m)

Grade: 3; in adverse conditions/poor visibility 4

Walking Time: 3 hours

Accommodation & Parking:

Wooler - hotels, inns, B/Bs, caravan/camping, youth hostel. Specified off-road parking in upper Harthope; do not park beyond the notice at GR 953225, 1/2 mile (0.8km) prior to Langleeford Farm.

The Route: From the small road-bridge close to the parking areas, Hedgehope's conical mass instantly beckons. For here a finger post, *'Housey Crag 1/2 mile, Hedgehope Hill 2 1/2 miles'*, points south between wall and Butterwell Sike to a footbridge over Harthope Burn. Once

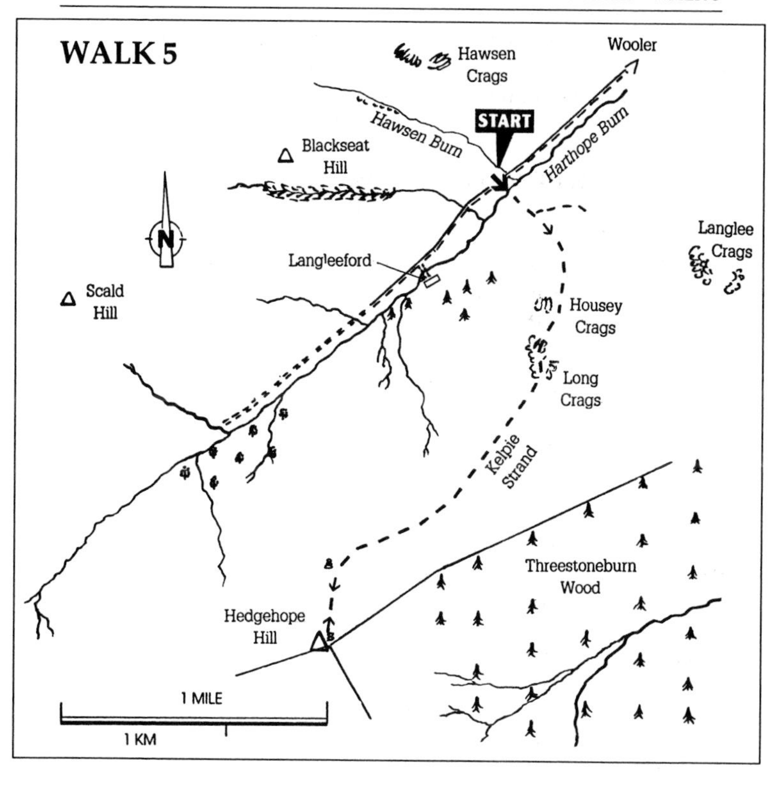

over the amber waters, ascend south, aided by waymarks, stiles and a permissive path that forks right to the towering mass of Housey Crags (1) with the outcropped ridge of Long Crags (1) beyond.

At the southerly end of Long Crag, the first of several waymarks assists passage, by peaty path, over the moorland wilderness of Kelpie Strand to the eastern, half conifer-clad flanks of Hedgehope Hill.

With the 'Scotsmans Heids' (cotton grass) and rush clumps of Kelpie Strand safely negotiated our way veers right on a narrow posted path climbing west, for now as the contours narrow the serious walking begins. Ahead, at the elbow in a broken fence turn left, i.e. south climbing alongside the intermittent and ageing fence posts, making for a solitary and sizeable cairn on the skyline ahead.

With bent grass and 'blaeberry' (bilberry) underfoot, leave the fence-line for the cairn from where a further marker post leads south to Hedgehope's untidy cap of wind shelters and summit stones (2). Standing at 2343ft (714m), the second highest in the Cheviot range, this superb grandstand immediately dispels any slight discomfort experienced during ascent. Rest and enjoy the sighing Cheviot winds and the grasses as they ebb and flow; I must however draw attention to the vagaries of Cheviot winds - at times they can be downright fractious.

Three fences meet on Hedgehope's summit, each leading the eye over landscapes of heather and tussock, stimulating and isolated, with little company save that of the moorland birds and hardy Blackface and Cheviot sheep. Over the Harthope valley to the north the scene is dominated by extensive and varied close-ups of Cheviot's riven southern quarter.

The return to the valley floor is by our outward route, a pleasing descent providing insights east and north of the Harthope valley, Hawsen Crags and the rounded dome of Cold Law beyond, with time to inspect and enjoy Long and Housey Crags.

ITEMS OF INTEREST ALONG THE WAY

(1) HOUSEY CRAGS & LONG CRAGS. Classic examples of the many outcrops of hardened Andesite surrounding the Cheviot massif and known as 'The Metamorphic Aureole'. They invariably run roughly north-west to south-east, having been fashioned by directional ice flows. Other crags, such as Langlee and Tathey, are nearby.

(2) HEDGEHOPE HILL - 'Head of the Valley'. For three points of the compass, the county's finest grandstand. To the east - Harthope valley, the coastal plain and the golden beaches guarded by the castles of Lindisfarne, Bamburgh, Dunstanburgh and Warkworth. Vistas south embrace Coquetdale, Rothbury Forest and Simonside to the haze of Tyneside; west is the Border Line astride the infinite, isolated allure of the Cheviot Hills/Range.

Walk 6: An Archaeological Adventure
BROUGH LAW, COCHRANE PIKE AND TURF KNOWE

Type of Walk: *A high level trek of discovery, with many manmade marks still in evidence, even after three thousand years of man's inconsideration for his heritage. A short but demanding journey, by waymarked hill paths and trods that provide not only a fine insight into the ways of those who passed before, but also, as with so many of Northumberland's walks, breathtaking views into the vastness of this border county.*

Maps: OS 1:25 000 Outdoor Leisure 16, The Cheviot Hills
OS 1:25 000 Pathfinder Series, NT 81/91
OS 1:50 000 Landranger, Sheet 81

Start/Finish: The National Park Bulby's Wood car park, GR 008164, 3/4 mile (1.2km) W from Ingram; which in turn stands 3 miles (4.6km) W from the A697 1 mile (1.6km) N of Powburn.

Distance: 5 miles (8km)

Height Gain: 1207ft (368m)

Grade: 2, if Brough Law presents no problems, 3 otherwise

Walking Time: 3 1/2 hours

Accommodation & Parking:
A range of accommodation, hotels to youth hostel, at Wooler; village and farmhouse B/Bs in the vicinity of Glanton and Powburn. Off-road parking Bulby's Wood car park, GR 008164.

The Route: Leave by crossing the road and on a broad grass track rise to the marker post on the small ridge ahead. Swing right with the grassy permissive path, marked in orange on the waymark posts and on the OS Outdoor Leisure map, ascending west to Brough Law (1). As height is gained evidence of early settlements can be seen - grassy mounds and hollows, rigg and furrowed fields - as our path skirts between conifers and gnarled thorn bushes by a broken wall. When the rocky outcrops are met pause, not only to refill the lungs, but also to admire the surrounding scenery, including the scree and gorse of Ewe Hill and the hound's tooth of Cunyan Crags to the north-west.

Continue climbing to the summit of Brough Law (1), surrounded by an extensive ring of defensive stones. From here the entire upper

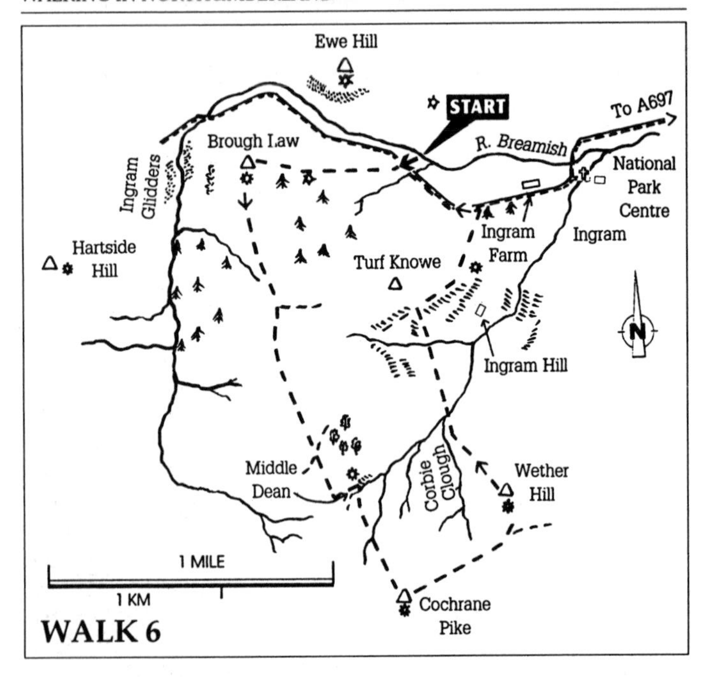

Breamish valley, a great basin of moorland grasses, opens up west to Cushat Law and High Cantle. Depart south, from this still proud Iron Age fort, via a grass, waymarked ('Breamish Valley Access Agreement to protect wildlife and farm animals, dogs should be kept on a lead on the access land and on permissive paths') track gradually descending towards the whitelands of a second Ewe Hill (2). At the first fork bear half right with the undulating path, south through furrowed moorland, ignoring incoming tracks, to follow the waymarks posted at intermittent intervals. An invigorating high way so typically Cheviot, and to the left, just beyond a deep-riven cleugh, one can see fine examples of medieval terracing.

With Little Cleugh approaching and cairned mounds surrounding, the way rises and falls, west of a clutch of sombre dark trees where a wire and post enclosure guides us south to Middle Dean and its overlooking hillfort (3). Cross the fence corner by stile to the prominent embankments of the fort, leaving it south via the dramatically pleasing steep-sided dean for a half-mile ascent to the grassy and yes, fort topped summit of Cochrane Pike. Although distinctly waymarked the permissive path south-south-east is in places ill-defined underfoot. A minor detail, for Cochrane Pike provides sightings of Northumberland's coastline and one of its castles, plus the splendid variations of its surrounding escarpments and high rising Cheviots.

Leave Cochrane at the multi-marker post walking approximately north-east by grass paths, crossing the waymarked whitelands of tussock and occasional patches of rush to the unmistakable and visibly fortified dome, ditches and embankments of Wether Hill (4). Just listen to the larks. Leave the airy top of Wether Hill treking north-north-west for a marker post below; distant Cunyan Crag's pointed rocks also provide a good marker. Further waymarks guide steeply down to the confluence of Corbie Cleugh and Middle Dean, on a bearing of 340° magnetic. This low point is left by gate to rise north over cultivation terraces marking the southern flanks of Turf Knowe to join the bridleway north-east above Ingram Hill. Ahead the scene is changing to valley pastoral, where man's flourishing presence in the Breamish valley through the ages is illustrated by further evidence of settlements and acres of terracing. The final descent to the valley floor and Bulby's Wood car park is by rutted cart track and the grassy verges of the valley road.

ITEMS OF INTEREST ALONG THE WAY

(1) BROUGH LAW 926ft (282m). A complete encircling wall, ditch and in places a second wall, with an internal circumference of 250 paces enclose this Iron Age fort. Gate gaps, one on the east side and what appears to be a recent one on the west side, can be seen, as can the foundations of three hut circles to the south.

(2) EWE HILL, WETHER HILL. No prizes for guessing the Cheviot Hills are prime sheep country, for so many landmarks carry the local terms referring to sheep (ewe - female sheep, wether - castrated ram/tup).

(3) MIDDLE DEAN HILLFORT. Surrounding embankments, ditches and internal hut remains are, even after two millennia, noticeable. For this fort, even though barely excavated, was likely to

be home to Iron Age man, who, as a result of a lowering of temperatures and deteriorating climate, was driven down from the higher settlements of his Bronze Age predecessors - though never into the valley floor for at that time valleys were invariably clothed in scrubby trees and ill-drained swamps.

(4) WETHER HILL. The summit fort and settlement, although not on such a scale as Yeavering Bell to the north, provides one of the county's finest examples of prehistoric architecture. Protective linear and circular earthworks, remains of internal hut foundations and surrounding rigg and furrow field cropping systems are evident.

WALK 7: The Great Breamish Round
INGRAM, LINHOPE, HIGH CANTLE and SALTER'S ROAD

Type of Walk: *A serious undertaking for energetic and well equipped walkers, encircling the ridgeways above the Breamish valley. The height gain of 2418ft (737m) is evenly spread throughout the walk and is never severe nor exposed. Passage underfoot varies from cart tracks and grassy bridleways to heather tangled trods, producing a variety of views, frequent sightings of upland wildlife and evidence galore of those who have peopled this unique place for the last 8000 years.*

Maps: OS 1:25 000 Outdoor Leisure 16, The Cheviot Hills
OS 1:25 000 Pathfinder Series, NT 81/91
OS 1:50 000 Landranger, Sheet 81

Start/Finish: From Ingram Haughs, GR 020165, prior to Ingram Bridge, 3 miles (4.6km) W from the A697, 1 mile (1.6km) N of Powburn.

Distance: 16¾ miles (26.8km)

Height Gain: 2418ft (737m)

Grade: 4

Walking Time: 8 hours

Accommodation & Parking:
Wooler, ranging from hotels to youth hostel. Limited range in Glanton and Powburn. Off-road parking on Ingram Haughs, GR 020164.

Foot of Breamish and head of Till
Meet together at Bewick Mill.

Anon.

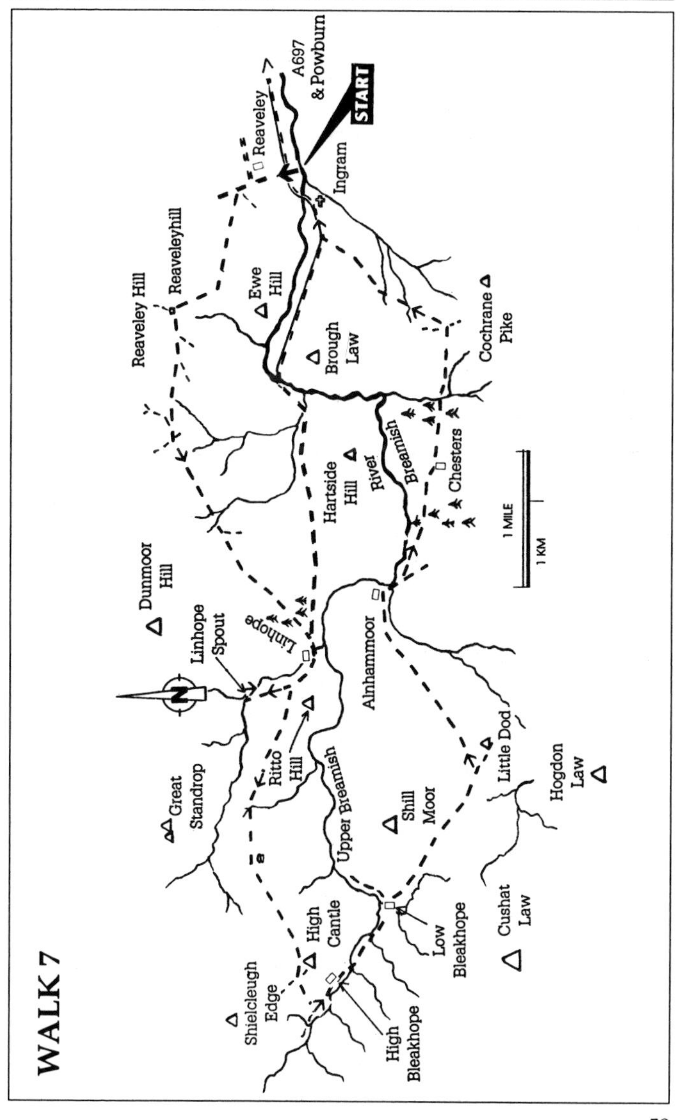
WALK 7
START
A697
& Powburn
Reaveley
Ingram
Reaveleyhill
Reaveley Hill
Ewe
Hill
Brough
Law
Cochrane
Pike
Hartside
Hill
River
Breamish
Chesters
1 MILE
1 KM
Dunmoor
Hill
Linhope
Spout
Linhope
Alnhammoor
Great
Standrop
Ritto
Hill
Upper Breamish
Shill
Moor
Little Dod
Hogdon
Law
Cushat
Law
Low
Bleakhope
High
Cantle
Shielcleugh
Edge
High
Bleakhope

The Route: The Ingram Haughs (1) (flat riverside pastures) provide a gentle start to this high level trek over the Breamish heights. Walk north with the lane past the T-junction by Reaveley Farm; 250yds beyond turn left, i.e. west with the public footpath post, 'Threestoneburn House'. Ascend the gated way, alongside pasture fences, to the ridge below Reaveley Hill. Then by ladder stile (a fine viewpoint) north-west to the abandoned moorland shieling of Reaveleyhill.

From the barn and crumbling shieling continue west via rutted cart track, making for the prominent and jagged Cunyan Crags of Dunmoor Hill (a visible part of the Metamorphic Aureole). Taking the right hand fork at each of the three forks along the way and keeping parallel with the right hand fence, cross the mire of Knock Burn's source on a thin trod rising to a bridleway waymark post ahead. Swing left with the bridleway for a scenic journey south-west, dominated by the valley's bastions of Shill Moor, Cushat Law and the long ridge of cairned Hogden Law. Passing below Cunyan Crags, by sheep pens, the grassed-over foundations of the medieval village and a second sheep fold and tin hut, the way is criss-crossed by paths and tracks bisecting our route. Ignore them all and once through the gated stone wall, swing half left, i.e. south-south-west between two coniferous plantations and onto the gated cart track, descending to the picturesque community of Linhope below the prehistoric village of Greaves Ash.

Continue with the winding lane over Linhope Burn, rising with the waymarks north-west to Linhope Spout (2); noting, alongside the rising cart track, a bridleway sign directing left (we return to this point to continue our journey after a visit to Linhope Spout). Although the detour north by permissive path to Linhope Spout adds 1 mile (1.6km) it would be remiss not to visit this most spectacular of Cheviot waterfalls.

Returning to the bridleway ascend the cart track west-north-west by Ritto Hill, passing the grassed over foundations of a medieval settlement, to cross a waymarked two-step stile for a journey north-west to the dour ridged wilderness over Rig Cairn. A trek that is dominated to the north by Hedgehope Hill and its outlyer the twin outcropped Great Standrop. Pass through an unmarked field-gate, rising by a deteriorating grass track through

Linhope Spout in spate

heather, overlooking the upper Breamish valley, to the ridge above the great cleft of Carswell Cleugh. The public bridleway marked on the OS map traverses rough ill-defined heather trods north-west - bearing 300° magnetic - then west - bearing 272° magnetic - by the prominent Rig Cairn and finally from GR 940169 north of Rig Cairn, swing south-west - bearing 242° magnetic - to High Cantle via a waymarked wicket gate at GR 929163. The gate leads north-west i.e. right through a tangle of heather to a gated boundary fence prior to descending steeply west-south-west, by waymark posts, into the cleugh scarred Upper Breamish Valley (3).

Turn left and walk south-east with the farm lane, crossing the River Breamish beyond High Bleakhope Farm, one of Northumberland's most remote. At Low Bleakhope Farm, the river and its accompanying farm lane squeeze left between steep skirts of Low Cantle and Shill Moor, whilst we ascend south-west via the old track of the Salter's Road (4). At the top of the gated pass between Shill Moor and Little Dod descend toward the grassy summit of Little Dod, then by waymarked public path leave Salter's Road left via an invigorating ridgeway north-east and east returning to the valley floor at Alnhammoor. Alive with the sounds and antics of moorland birds and bounding with mountain hares the way also provides views of the dark flanks of Ritto Hill by the sylvan enclave of Linhope.

Skirt by Alnhammoor Farm to cross the Breamish and follow the left, lower bridleway through pastures and Cobden plantation prior to the short sharp ascent to the Iron Age settlement at Chesters. Once past the settlement remains skirt the plantation to round the abandoned house of Chesters on its north side and proceed east through an enclosure to Chesters Burn plantation. The pathway through the conifers differs in position from the definitive bridleway shown on the OS map, and could in the future be altered to coincide with that shown on the map. *Should this occur strategically sighted waymarks will be displayed.*

Ascend east by thin trod above Ramshaw Burn to reach the walled plantation fringing the prominent earthworks of Middle Dean prehistoric fort. As directed by the markers pass through the stiled wall north-east, to begin the scenic descent above Ingram Hill, noting in particular the many cultivation terraces and rigged/

furrowed medieval fields fringing Turf Knowe. At the valley floor veer right past Ingram Farm to the National Park Centre. Well worth a visit. Final yards to journey's end are by Ingram Bridge to the riverside haughs.

ITEMS OF INTEREST ALONG THE WAY

(1) INGRAM. A name derived from 'angr' - eighth century old English for grassland. Its towered church with narrow windows is mainly twelfth and thirteenth century and its old school is now the Information Centre for Northumberland's National Park.

(2) LINHOPE SPOUT. The Cheviot's most winsome and largest waterfall cascades 56ft (17m) into a rocky basin surrounded by silver birch. In times of drought a pencil-thin plume, in times of spate a thunderous torrent whose boom can be heard at Linhope.

(3) UPPER BREAMISH VALLEY. Gouged by ice and channelled by the River Breamish, rising on Scotsman's Knowe by Cheviot, this burn, the only one from Cheviot to be recognised as 'River', squirms by Quickening Cleugh, Bleakhope, Sniffies Scar and Snout End, eventually to lose its proud name to the River Till at Bewick.

(4) SALTER'S ROAD. This ancient trackway, first known as the 'Thief's Road', changed its name to 'Salter's Road' when salt was carried by packhorse, through the Cheviots, from the River Tyne into the Scottish Borders. An activity that no doubt created as many problems, for the Excise men, as did the 'Thief's Road'.

Walk 8: Ancient Ways through *'Lytle Hills and Dyvers Valyes'*

RIVER ALWIN, KIDLAND FOREST and CLENNELL STREET

Type of Walk: *Aptly described in* A Survey of the Waste Lands, 1541: *'All the said Kydlande is full of lytle hills or mountaynes and dyvers valyes in which descende litle Ryvelles into a broke called Kydlande water [River Alwin] which falleth into the rever of Cokette nere to Alyntoun.' Little has changed underfoot, except the forests of Kidland and Kidlandlee now clothe 5½ miles (9km) of our walk. Waymarks are present on public footpaths, bridleways and concessionary ways. Length and ascents should not deter, for the rewards are high.*

Maps:	OS 1:25 000 Outdoor Leisure 16, The Cheviot Hills OS 1:50 000 Landranger Sheet 80, The Cheviot Hills
Start/Finish:	Alwinton, GR 921063, the last village in Coquet Dale, 9 miles (14.4km) NW of Rothbury.
Distance:	12½ miles (20km)
Height Gain:	1673ft (510m)
Grade:	4
Walking Time:	6½ hours
Accommodation & Parking:	Alwinton and Clennell Hall. Car park (free) in Alwinton.

The Route: Walk east past Alwinton's (1) Rose and Thistle crossing the village green and Hosedon Burn, via two 'Clennell Street' signs. Swing left past farm buildings rising north with the wide track of Clennell Street (2) to beyond Castle Hills. With the Hills' rippled dome on the left and a dual waymarked post right leave Clennell Street by stile for a blue ridgeway north; a route that provides inviting views of the silver ribboned River Alwin, Cushat Law and beyond to Cheviot.

Enter the conifers at the grassy valley floor, GR 920092, beneath the distinctive dome of the Dodd and Kitty's Crag, and walk north with the forest road. A way strewn with crumbling stone sheep stells, indicators that the forest was once sheep-country. Ahead, as the trees recede from the trackway, a wooden bothy, complete with stove, by the gated entrance to Kidland Forest (3) is met, marking the point where the jinking valley tightens its grip between lodgepole pine and larch. Continue with the valley road as Inner Hill spills down to the valley floor, to the ford over Yoke Burn, GR 918116.

Hopefully the burn will not be in spate, for at the waymarked fork 50yds/m ahead a choice greets the walker: left with a bridleway to sedately ascend forest tracks, via Heigh, to GR 911130 above Lindhope Linn; or right with the forest road to the confluence of Sting Burn and Yoke Burn, alongside the overgrown remains of Memmer Kirk (4), and then by a narrow, rising public path through the conifers to join the bridleway at GR 911130. Both routes are waymarked and of similar length as shown on the OS Outdoor Leisure map.

The route from GR 911130 leaves the forest track to travel

Ruined Castle, Hepburn (Walk 10)
Coe Crags, Thrunton (Walk 11)

Simonside Hills (Walk 14)
Deadwater Fell (Walk 15)

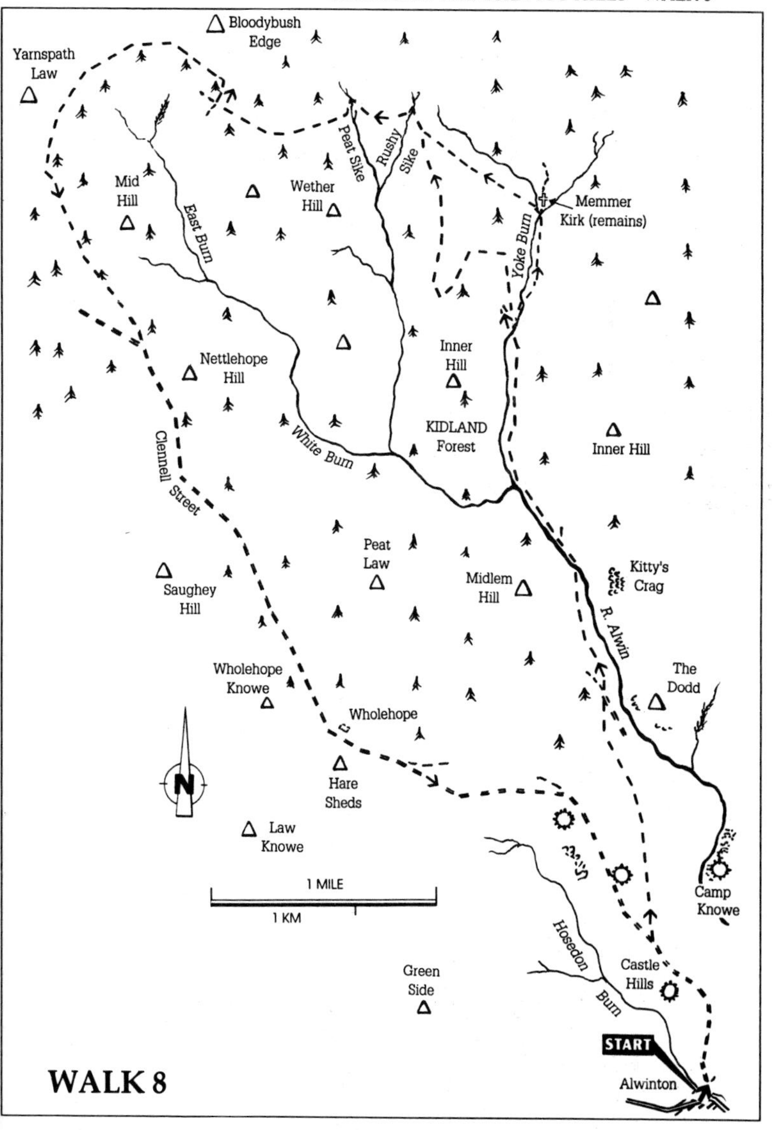
Bloodybush
Edge
Yarnspath
Law
Mid
Hill
East Burn
Peat Sike
Rushy
Sike
Wether
Hill
Memmer
Kirk (remains)
Yoke Burn
Nettlehope
Hill
Inner
Hill
KIDLAND
Forest
Inner Hill
Clennell
Street
White Burn
Peat
Law
Midlem
Hill
Kitty's
Crag
Saughey
Hill
R. Alwin
Wholehope
Knowe
The
Dodd
Wholehope
Hare
Sheds
N
Law
Knowe
1 MILE
1 KM
Camp
Knowe
Hosedon
Burn
Green
Side
Castle
Hills
START
Alwinton
WALK 8

basically west and later north-west for 1¼ miles (2km) through waymarked rides, crossing the mires of Rushy Sike and Peat Sike, to a major cross-rides at GR 903132. A way that does not always coincide with the bridleway as shown on the OS Outdoor Leisure map, it is however clear on the ground albeit at times via a faint path. At the airy cross-rides, with pleasing views and a feeling that the open fells are at hand, turn right, i.e. north for 250yds / m to burst out below the weeping hags and rounded summit of Bloodybush Edge, 2001ft (610m), named after some long forgotten border incident.

Turn sharp left following the thin trod north-west and west between forest edge and perimeter fence for a total release onto heather moorland by stile at GR 895139. Continue west to the fence ahead and as a moorland track is met turn left to rise south-west towards the summit ridge of Yarnspath Law, a stretch that provides superb views of the mottled southern face of Cheviot and the Border ridge, 3 miles (6km) north, over the whitegrassed slopes of Bloodybush Edge. At the corner of the plantation the path veers south, remaining on the moorland side of the perimeter fence, not entering the trees as is shown on the Outdoor Leisure map. Descend along the fenceline below Yarnspath Law for ¼ mile (0.4km) to the rush-ridden source of West Burn. Here a two-stepped stile (waymarked permissive footpath) takes us back into the trees and onto a forest road south, i.e. right.

This cheerful rolling road of ¾ mile (1.25km) surges through the conifers to emerge below Nettlehope Hill at the waymarked and gated Clennell Street junction. Welcomed by the rolling hills and winding valleys of Upper Coquetdale, spurred on by the delights of descending Clennell Street and inspired by the Northumbrian scenery to the crags of Simonside, make the final 5 miles (8km) to Alwinton an unforgettable experience. Pass as we walk betwixt forest and moorland, tussock clad Saughey Hill, the ruins of Wholehope (5) and signs of our prehistoric and medieval forebears in the remains of settlements, dykes and forts on Hosedon and Castle Hills.

ITEMS OF INTEREST ALONG THE WAY

(1) ALWINTON. Pronounced 'Allenton', an Anglian 'ton' or settlement by the River Alwin, thought to stand nearer to the

Norman church of St Michael (enlarged in the thirteenth century) at Low Alwinton. The highest village in Coquetdale, standing at the junction of ancient trails and drove roads, Alwinton was in early times the major settlement of the 'ten towns of Coquet Dale'.

(2) CLENNELL STREET. A medieval trade and drove way, leading south over the border line from Cocklawfoot, via Yarnspath Law, to Alwinton; it was then known as 'magnum viam de Yarnspeth'.

(3) KIDLAND. In 1181, the Cistercian abbey of Newminster, near Morpeth, assigned 'Kydlande to the south as far as the great road of Yarnspeth by the wood to Yarnspeth Burn' to monks and their servants for the grazing of sheep. A practice that produced the couplet in praise of Kidland's sheep, shepherds and dogs:

At Milkhope, Dryhope and Liland Lea
Their value is well known.

(4) MEMMER KIRK. Now a total ruin, this Middle Ages chapel was built for the devotions of the monks from Newminster Abbey, when 'summering' their extensive flocks of sheep in Kidland. It is said that life was so lonely for one of Memmer Kirk's chaplains that he made a bee-hive every day of the week. Excavations have revealed that Memmer Kirk was also a medieval longhouse (farmer, stock and all, housed under the same roof).

(5) WHOLEHOPE. 'Wool-up' in the local dialect; this one time shepherd's shieling and latterly a youth hostel is now, as are so many others, a sad ruin providing little else save shelter for sheep and fine views over middle Coquetdale.

Walk 9: Vintage Cheviots

COQUET VALLEY, BARROW LAW, WINDY GYLE to THE STREET

Type of Walk: *One of the finest of Cheviot walks, incorporating classic Cheviot ridge walking and far-seeing English/Scottish panoramas, coupled with incomparable Upper Coquet Dale. Two sharpish ascents and miles of waymarked grassy ridge paths populated by a host of wildlife and local sheep provide a rewarding, not too exhausting challenge that is best tackled on a clear day.*

Maps: OS 1:25 000 Outdoor Leisure 16, The Cheviot Hills
OS 1:50 000 Landranger Sheet 80, The Cheviot Hills

Start/Finish: Wedder Leap car park/picnic area, GR 866104, in Upper Coquet Dale 6 miles (9.6km) NW from Alwinton.

Distance: 9¼ miles (14.8km)

Height Gain: 1470ft (448m)

Grade: 3, in adverse weather/visibility 4

Walking Time: 5 hours

Accommodation & Parking:
Limited accommodation at Alwinton and Clennell. Parking at Wedder Leap car park/picnic area 300yds/m S of Barrowburn.

The Coquet for ever
The Coquet for aye;
The Coquet, the King
Of the bank and the brae.

Anon.

The Route: Walk north from the car park for 550yds (500m), alongside the road above the sparkling Coquet passing Barrowburn Farm. As the valley road angles left turn sharp right through a field gate, by a finger post 'Bridleway, Middle Hill and Border Ridge' onto a wallside cart track for 100yds/m. Here, at the corner of the farm buildings, a marker post indicates our 'blue' route ascending sharp left, i.e. north, through a second field gate to zigzag onto the skirts of Barrow Law. Behind is the great mass of cairn-topped Shillhope Law and below left, the folding fells of Upper Coquet Dale and the silver ribbon of the Coquet; with ahead, the great upland prairie of Cheviot 'Whitelands' (1).

Underfoot, a dry grass path puts a spring in the step as it surges north by Barrow Law and over Barrow ridge towards the mottled whale-back of muckle Cheviot. Domed hills, probing ridges, steep-sided valleys, all favoured by trilling larks, indicate this is Cheviot country, just as timber fringed Yarnspath Law (2) signals that Usway Burn and the lonely farm of Uswayford (3) are in the valley below. All too soon the pine green finger of Murder Cleugh (does anyone know the details of how this cleugh got its gory name?) and its accompanying dirt road are passed. Cross onto a thin bridlepath rising north then north-north-east over the grassy flanks of Ward Law.

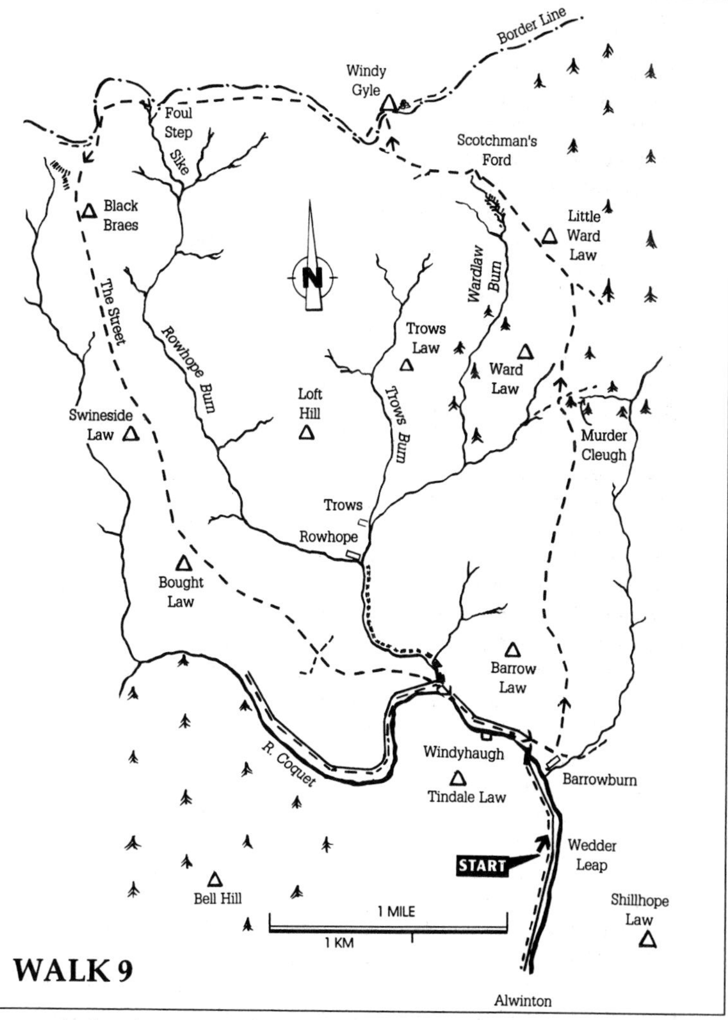

WALK 9

As height is gained and a twin track path crossed east of the flattened cone of Ward Law, the now distinct way veers north-west to clip the tip of Little Ward Law. Ahead Windy Gyle beckons over

River Coquet through Upper Coquet Dale

the scarred cleugh head of Scotsman's Ford, and as ascent steepens dual directional markers assist the final yards. Note the permissive path marker directing north by rutted trod, away from the bridleway to Windy Rig, to the summit tumulus of Windy Gyle (4).

From this windy eyrie progress west and south for a delightful journey, via the Pennine Way and The Street (5); do not be deterred by unappetising placenames, such as Foul Step or The Slime, met en route. Descend with the well-worn Pennine Way to cross the watershed col of well-named Windy Rig, noting the shapely, jinking cleughs surrounding Rowhope Burn and Foulstep Sike as the rippling way negotiates the 'floating waters' of Foul Step to join The Street at Plea Knowe below Mozie Law.

Guided south and finally south-east, by the finger post 'Bridleway, The Street, Coquet Valley 3 miles', the waymarked ridge undulates over Black Braes (5), Swineside Law and Hindside Knowe prior to dropping into the twists of Coquet Dale. This fine ridgeway follows partially visible packhorse and drove tracks above the distinctive and dramatic valleys of Carlcroft and Rowhope. Although the temptation to wander is high, do stick to the path as the surrounds are Dry Training Areas used by the MOD. At the valley road cross the bridge over Rowhope Burn, where, in the

1700s, stood an inn whose 'spirit' came from illicit sources hidden in the surrounding cleughs. Join the musical Coquet and the valley road as they squeeze south-east between Barrow Law and Tindale Law.

End this Cheviot experience with the best roadside walk in the book, as Windyhaugh (6) and Barrowburn are passed on the return to the car park and picnic area.

ITEMS OF INTEREST ALONG THE WAY

(1) WHITELANDS. The local name for vast areas of matgrass *(nardus stricta)* covering the ridges and upper slopes of the Cheviot range. The grass produces in June an erect spike, which as autumn approaches bleaches almost white, hence 'Whitelands'.

(2) YARNSPATH LAW. Mentioned in a medieval charter describing Clennell Street, 'magnum viam de Yarnspath'.

(3) USWAYFORD. A typical outlying hill farm, one of the 'last in England', it is 3 miles from the nearest tarmac road and 10 miles from the nearest village / inn. During severe winters it can be cut off for long periods, as experienced in 1940-41 when it was isolated for 17 weeks. Today it provides welcome B/B accommodation for pennine wayfarers.

(4) WINDY GYLE 2032ft (619m). Fourth in the Cheviot's pecking order, commanding splendid views into England (Lakeland and Cross Fell) and Scotland. The Bronze Age tumulus (now an untidy pile) capping its summit is known as 'Russell's Cairn', in memory of Sir Francis Russell who was shot, not on this precise spot but some distance to the east, during a Border altercation in 1585.

(5) THE STREET. Named as 'The Clattering Path' on General Roy's map of 1775, this high level drove road runs from Hownam in Roxburghshire, over the Border, onto Black Braes and Upper Coquet Dale. Gouged trenches south of Black Braes indicate driven cattle and the passage of packhorses. Black Braes 'Cross Dykes' are thought to be medieval earthworks, to block or restrict the passage of 'reived stock'.

(6) WINDYHAUGH. Once a mill for the monks of Newminster, the building west of the present farmhouse was the original farm and upper dale's school.

CHAPTER 2
Crags and Dales

Oh, my heart is fain to hear the soft wind blowing,
Soughing through the tree tops up on northern fells.
Oh, my eye's an ache to see the brown burns flowing
Through the peaty soil and tinkling heather bells.

Ada Smith

Northumberland's geological evolution has left it greatly blessed with 'the bank and the brae', for its many dales and their rocky guardians of great whin-sill or weather worn outcrops of fell-sandstone can be seen and enjoyed throughout the length and breadth of the county. The walker is offered a varied and scenic choice of wild walking, craggy ascents, forest treks and gentle riverside strolls; through dales that have few equals, where infant burns foam and froth in winter spate, turning at lower levels into the musical waters of summer, song and verse.

Dales, burns and rivers, in places heavily clothed with regimented conifer, wind and widen in harmony through Northumberland's upland prairies and pastoral plains, all from source to sea within the county save for the River South Tyne. It rises at Tynehead above Garrigill in Cumbria then by sandstone step flows into Northumberland by Randleholme Tower north of Alston.

The Cheviot marks the source of the most northerly burns, rivers and valleys of Chapter 2, all flowing from its spongy summit to join the River Till, above whose valley Ros Castle and Hepburn Crags stand guard. A second river from Cheviot's outlyers, the River Aln, runs through the Vale of Whittingham to Alnwick, and by sweeping horseshoes to the North Sea at Alnmouth.

The River Coquet through Coquetdale, the most captivating in the county, traverses Northumberland from west to east to spill its amber waters into the North Sea by Warkworth and Amble. Little wonder this guide contains five walks alongside or within sight of this majestic dale.

From Coquethead journey south-west over the dour lands of Redesdale, to the county boundary with Scotland at Deadwater, from whose uncertain watershed the northern leg of Northumberland's greatest river, the River North Tyne flows. Prompting A.C. Swinburne, in *A Jacobite's Exile*, to pen,

But bonnier shine the braes of Tyne
Than a' the fields of France.

An unpredictable river, much given to winter and spring spates through wild and lonely North Tyne Dale, its moods and those of the dales are now softened by Kielder's mighty reservoir and all embracing cloak of conifers. Beyond Bellingham, fed by Tarset Burn and later the River Rede, its surrounds soften as it winds to the meeting of the waters with the River South Tyne at Warden Rocks above Hexham. Now as one the River Tyne flows east through industrial Tyneside to Tynemouth, becoming en route 'The Tyne, the Tyne, the Coaly Tyne'.

The most southerly of all Northumberland's dales are the wild and mine-scarred East and West Allen Dales. Marching with both Durham and Cumbria the county boundary skims the sources of their rivers, above Allenheads village and the pitted remains of Coalcleugh mines. Both dales prospered in the eighteenth century, the result of lead and silver rich deposits beneath the moorland peat, a bonanza that faded in the mid 1800s to leave a scatter of mining memorabilia and a legacy of miner's tracks and carrier's ways. Sweeping open moorland gives way to stocked enclosures and parkland beyond Whitfield where the two Allens meet to surge through the tree clad cliffs of Staward Crags and Allen Gorge prior to spilling into the River South Tyne east of Bardon Mill.

THE WALKS

Walks 10 to 27 explore Northumberland's crags and dales, listed not by individual dales but, as in keeping with Chapters I and 3, in a north to south progression; beginning with an ascent to Ros Castle, that is not a castle, but from where seven of Northumberland's finest can be seen. **Walk 11**, high above Aln Vale, rises above Callaly Crags to traverse the spectacular Long Crag and Coe Crags; whilst the short but scenically spectacular **Walk 12** visits not only the massive Drake Stone and a dark talking tarn, but also the banks of the Coquet. **Walk 13** also gazes over green and pleasant Coquetdale, as it winds through woods from a holy place to Fairy Glen; with **Walk 14** we climb to Simonside Crags (seen from every quarter of Northumberland) high above the sweeping curves of the Coquet. **Walk 15** introduces North Tynedale, Kielder Forest and Kielder Water reservoir in a big way, with an ascent of Peel Fell and a visit to the Kielder Stane; and for those who love a challenge **Walk 16** provides the Kielder Water Marathon.

For those who prefer a short, scenic burnside journey of high interest I would suggest **Walk 17** by Tarset Burn in North Tynedale. **Walk 18**, the first of the Wallington walks, encircles the higher ground of Greenleighton to Fontburn Reservoir whilst Wallington's Wannie Line, **Walk 19**, takes a railbed circuit from Scot's Gap above the River Wansbeck and west of Rothley Crags. **Walk 20** from a lakeside start rises imperceptibly to the classic crags and silver birch of Shaftoe south of Wansbeck vale. **Walk 21** heralds a change of crag and dale, from the pastoral peace of Wansbeck to the ups and downs, in wind and sun, of Hadrian's Wall running with the great whin-sill crags north of South Tynedale. **Walk 22** is a linear journey through the keyhole of Allen Gorge on the southern aspect of South Tynedale, a fascinating waterside and ridge journey; leading to **Walk 23**, a rail and fragrant riverside circuit of style and tranquillity by Lambley Viaduct and the River South Tyne.

Walk 24 takes us into the adjoining charismatic lead and silver dales of East and West Allen Dale from Allendale Town to the flues and chimney stacks on the ridge above. **Walk 25** skips a dale into Derwentdale on the county boundary to trek the moorland ways of drover, miner and monk, with **Walk 26** returning to explore the county's Klondyke in wild West Allendale. The chapter ends at the county's most southerly village, Allenheads, alpha & omega of **Walk 27**, for an in-depth, on-foot experience of the life and times of the lead miner.

Walk 10: Castles Ahoy
ROS CASTLE and HEPBURN MOOR

Type of Walk: *A circular crag and moorland adventure, uniquely Northumbrian, skirting the rugged grandeur of the sandstone escarpment above Chillingham Castle; visiting Bronze Age forts, a hill top from which seven of Northumbria's great castles can be seen, and a moor that demands map reading skills. Underfoot, paths vary from waymarked moorland and woodland tracks to undefined, barely discernible, fell trods. Choose a clear day for a kaleidoscope of distant views and upland wildlife.*

Maps: OS 1:25 000 Pathfinder 476, Chatton & Eglingham
OS 1:50 000 Landranger Sheet 75, Berwick-upon-Tweed

Start/Finish: Hepburn Woods, Forest Enterprise car park and picnic area, GR 072248, 3½ miles (5.6km) S and signposted E from Chatton. Chatton is 5 miles (8km) E from Wooler via the B6348.

Distance: 7 miles (11.2km)

Height Gain: 919ft (280m)

Grade: 3

Walking Time: 3½ hours

Accommodation & Parking:
Inn and B/Bs in and around Chatton. Wider range available in Wooler. Parking (free) in Hepburn Woods car park, GR 072248.

The Route: Leave the car park, picnic benches and information board, walking east with the orange arrowheads, our guides to Ros Castle and through Ros Hill Wood, courtesy of Forest Enterprise's Ros Castle walk. Almost immediately swing left, between whin and broom, rising through larch and pine onto the bracken and heather clad Hepburn Crags. Veer right ascending south-east, via a choice of zigzags through the awesome outcrops, to the perimeter embankments of Hepburn Crag Fort (1).

A marked path cuts through the bracken infested fort, east/north-east over the heathery acres of Hepburn Moor on a wide pathway, below a sprinkling of caledonian pine, aiming for the prominent, half tree-clad hill of Ros Castle (2). At the roadway cross to a marker-post indicating the winding ascent over the flared,

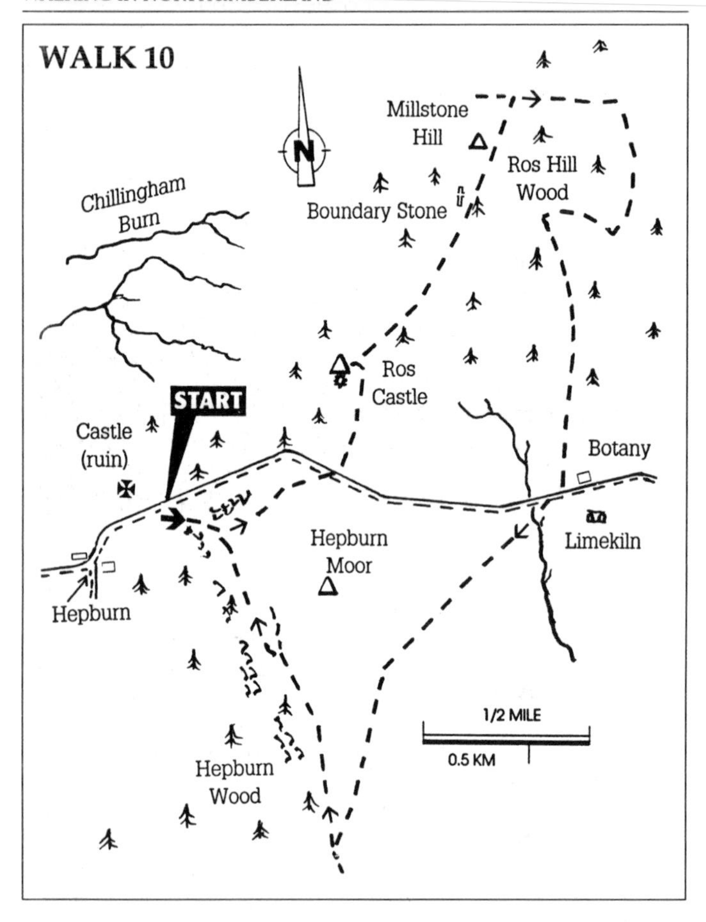

bracken clad skirts to the heathery bell-shaped dome of Ros Castle. What appears to be a stiff climb turns out to be just the opposite as the final feet to the triangulation pillar are helped by a stepped pathway.

Leave the summit north-north-east, descending alongside Chillingham Castle's (3) boundary wall, initially over moorland to a wicket gate at Shepherd's Cairn; here the way plunges between

Limekiln, Hepburn Moor

stands of conifers on either side of the continuing wall. Views however are not excluded - particularly pleasing is the shapely nab of Chattonpark Hill above the River Till to the north. At the point where Chillingham Wall angles left note the small boundary stone left of the pathway, marked 'T 1859' and 'N 1859' on opposing faces (T - Tankerville Estate and N - Duke of Northumberland's land). Continue to the orange arrowhead finger post pointing right, i.e. east through the conifers of Ros Hill Wood.

A waymarked woodland journey, with chattering finches and clattering cushats, of 1¾ miles (2.8km), through wide rides and forest fringes, passes the heathery summit of Willie's Law to meander south onto fell and pasture. Here a grass track continues south, by stone heaps and pine plantation, guiding the feet to the moorland road by Botany Farm and the eye to the long stony ridge capped by the blip of Blawearie. With Botany left and a conspicuous limekiln ahead, turn right onto the roadside for 70yds/m to a fingerpost 'Public Footpath Blawearie 2½ miles', our marker for a wilderness traverse left over Hepburn Moor.

Surrounded by endless moorland and sandstone scattered ridges follow a course of 230° magnetic, over the rushes of sluggish

Harehope Burn on ill-defined trods, through a clutch of 'bell pits/ sink holes' (limestone perhaps?) and a rushy mire, to a crumbling shieling at GR 083241. At its ruined walls and wooden pole, veer half left, 205° magnetic, rising to the ridge top on an improving trod for 1000yds (1km) to meet a public footpath coming in from the right. With Hedgehope Hill and Cheviot massif visible west over the Till valley, turn sharp right above the wooded scarp of Hepburn Moor, walking north.

A picturesque return of 1 mile (1.6km), in parallel with the perimeter silver birches and fence of Hepburn Wood, leads through the fort above Hepburn Crags. If you wish, join Forest Enterprise's 'Red Walk' north as it opens onto the moorland, by a wicket gate from Hepburn Wood at GR 077241. Beyond the fort descend through the scattered sandstone blocks, with views of ruined Hepburn Castle, for a marked return to the car park and picnic area.

ITEMS OF INTEREST ALONG THE WAY

(1) HEPBURN CRAG FORT. One of many Bronze Age forts/ camps/settlements overlooking the Till valley and Milfield Plain; typified by an elliptical rampart, in some cases up to 15ft (4.5m) in height, surrounding earthworks, ditches and offset gateways.

(2) ROS CASTLE - 1034ft (315m). Capped by a Bronze Age hillfort, this prominent hill served during the Border Wars as a warning beacon; verified by Sir Robert Bowes's Report to the Marquis of Dorset, 1551, 'The Lord Evers claymed from the confynes of Berwick, that all villages in that quarter were contributary to the fyending of the beacon at Rawes Castle.' The summit pillar bears a commemorative plaque to Viscount Grey of Falloden, naturalist and Foreign Minister, whose favourite view point it was. Wide and far ranging views include the Cheviot massif and seven of the county's greatest castles: Chillingham, Ford, Lindisfarne, Bamburgh, Dunstanburgh, Warkworth and Alnwick. Four informative directional indicators are positioned on a small stone summit platform.

(3) CHILLINGHAM CASTLE. Originally a four towered fourteenth century Northumbrian stronghold held by the Heron family, then the Greys, second only to the Percys in the Northumbrian pecking order. Seventeenth century rebuilding enlarged the castle and in the

early eighteenth century it became the seat of the Earls of Tankerville. Chillingham Park is home to England's last herd of genuine wild cattle, a strain of wild 'white' cattle that has remained pure for 700 years. The park surrounds (James Knott Trust) and castle (National Trust) are worth a visit in their own right.

Walk 11: By Forest, Fell & Craggy Ridge
THRUNTON WOODS, CALLALY CRAGS to LONG CRAG and COE CRAGS

Type of Walk: *Forest, heather moorland and craggy ridge combine to create a circular adventure of discovery for the enthusiast and the young at heart. Red-waymarked paths and upland tracks reveal a profusion of forest and fell wildlife, centuries of history and some of the county's finest views. If time does not allow a complete circuit, diversions or shorter circular walks are possible.*

Maps: OS 1:50 000 Landranger Sheet 81, Alnwick & Morpeth
OS 1 Inch to 1 Statute Mile, Alnwick

Start/Finish: Thrunton Woods, Forest Enterprise car park/picnic area, GR 085097. 1½ miles (2.4km) N from the A697 at GR 098062, 15 miles (24km) SSE from Wooler.

Distance: 10¾ miles (17.2km)

Height Gain: 1706ft (520m)

Grade: 3, due to steep ascents and length. No navigational problems

Walking Time: 5½-6 hours

Accommodation & Parking:
The market town of Rothbury provides a variety of accommodaton. Park at Forest Enterprise Thrunton Woods car park.

The 'Red' Route: From the car park information board walk to the road, turning left, i.e. north with the waymarked lane. Curving west with the forest fence, by the 'Rothbury Forest' noticeboard, pass through a kissing gate onto the stony track streaking south-west below Thrunton Crags.

Halfway along this straight forest road, at a vehicle turning-point, a marked needle-strewn trod zigzags left. Climb through rhododendrons, silver birch and conifer to Wedderburn's Hole (1),

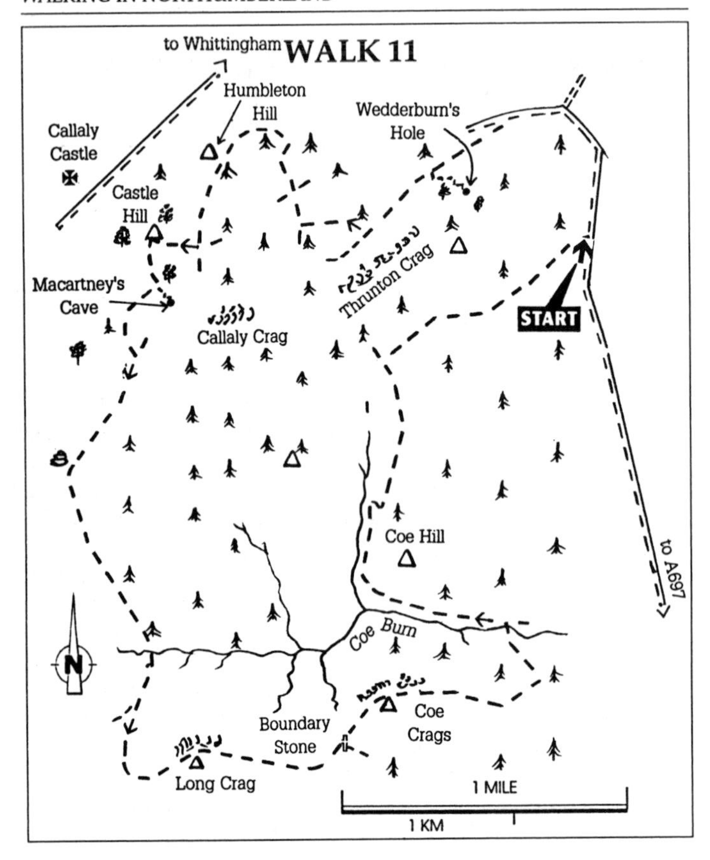

amidst a jumble of fallen rocks, identified by an indicator board and the initials 'T W' (the W tilted obliquely) carved on the cave-side rock. *The narrow entrance should be observed, not entered.* Return to the forest road below and immediately turn left.

Rhododendron, broom, rowan and larch decorate this road, and by the large rhododendrons on the right leave the road with the waymarks - *this right turn is not as shown on the 'Forests of Rothbury Walks' leaflet.* Crossing a drainage ditch on a stone footbridge, swing left by stately pine, home to clattering cushats, while underfoot seams of old red sandstone surface as a wide T-junction, with grand views of Thrunton and Callaly Crags, is reached.

Turn right, with the red waymarks, eventually ascending left and left again to skirt the trees and scrub of Humbleton Hill, much favoured by finches (2), chats and swallows, to link again with the orange route below Castle Hill. Veer right through the drystone wall (3), rising through rhododendron and silver birch with bilberry underfoot, to the contorted beech and sandstone crowning Castle Hill's sun-dappled earthworks. Leave this prehistoric site with the red / orange markers, dropping through Scots pine to a single-step fence stile directing right.

A short diversion, signposted Macartney's Cave (4), rises between weather-worn rocks, one of which contains The Cave. Return with care and follow the fence north, leaving it to ascend left, emerging via the stony defile of Hob's Nick (5) onto Callaly Crag. *For a shorter circuit follow the orange route left from Hob's Nick. For the energetic divert to a solitary orange marker post on the open fell, turning left via a heathery trod to the sandstone viewpoint on Callaly Crag. Return to Hob's Nick.*

From the junction the red route, now a permissive path, trundles south-west through sparse Scots pine and tangled heather. Ahead, a prominent pile of stones on the plateau shoulder beckons. They are tumulus stones, one of many burial cairns / cists on the surrounding fells, crudely arranged into a rough shelter. The burial mound does however provide grandstand views of this picturesque quadrant of Northumberland.

The pathway south passes through a gate to Forestry land, sloping to Coe Burn below the black barrier of Long Crag's north face. Another leads to the infant burn, beyond which a third brings the walker to within 130 paces of the ribbon of peat climbing south, upwards of 427ft (130m), to the cairn of Long Crag. An easier ascent than first thought.

The cairn, with wonderful views, leads to Long Crag's triangulation pillar - 1048ft (319m), today's high point; geologists and scramblers may find the sandstone crags, some 30yds / m north of the pillar, of unusual interest. Scramble down between outcrops to the first step and at the eastern end of the crags examine the patterns and profiles of the coloured, sculptured rock, exhibiting a honeycomb / netting effect in bas-relief.

Journey east to Coe Crags, on the wide slash of peat and sandstone through heather, noting the boundary stones. At the T-junction, flanked with boundary stones (6) veer left, then left again at the next fork, dropping and rising through a barren stand of burnt larch to Coe Crags - 1007ft (307m). This grandstand, gazing east over Alnwick Moor to the North Sea, is left on a narrowing descending red path into and through the bracken infested tree-line, finally crossing the tinkling Coe Burn by wooden footbridge onto a forest road.

Turn left onto the contouring ash track, rising west and north around the tree-clad flanks of Coe Hill for 1 mile (1.6km), watched over by the craggy north face of Coe and Long Crags. The returning waymarked route, by Black Walter, north, east then north-east is by forest tracks and roads, allowing time to look out for wildlife, as the way slopes through the tall lodgepole pine to the car park.

ITEMS OF INTEREST ALONG THE WAY

(1) WEDDERBURN'S HOLE. In this cave Thomas Wedderburn, a reiver from these parts, was run to ground and eventually died from gunshot wounds.

(2) CROSSBILL. A remarkable finch with an elongated and crossed bill, 'scissors', that are ideal for dealing with the hard seeds of conifers. Pine forests are greatly favoured, and great flocks of crossbills can be seen wheeling in from North-west Europe.

(3) DRYSTONE WALLERS. Each county has its own style of this skilled craft. Northumberland walls are based on the double wall principle, walls built on solid 'footings', leaning inwards and packed with 'chatter'/'fillings'. The whole is locked or keyed by a flat 'through stone' or 'thruff' and capped with a half-rounded 'capstone'.

(4) MACARTNEY'S CAVE. Fashioned by the hand of Macartney, a nineteenth century monk from Callaly Castle, it served as a solitary cell or retreat.

(5) HOB'S NICK. The name of this narrow defile reflects country superstitions, when the little people, such as Hobgoblins or 'Hobs', were blamed for numerous disasters.

(6) BOUNDARY STONES. Estate perimeters, under the Enclosures Acts of the 1700s and 1800s, were marked with inscribed stones. In

this case the four in the vicinity of the track junction all carry 'S' on one side, referring to Selby estate. Two carry 'A' on the reverse side, the third is blank and the fourth is imprinted 'N', for the Dukes of Northumberland.

Walk 12: Coquetdale's Millstones
THE DRAKE STONE & HARBOTTLE LOUGH

Type of Walk: *A walk of character, which although short, provides instant scenic variation, high interest and a plethora of Northumberland's indigenous wildlife. Underfoot, paths are moorland or forest tracks of heather-lined grass and peat, with occasional wet sections by Harbottle Lough. Waymarks assist over the open fell.*

Maps: OS 1:25 000 Outdoor Leisure 16, The Cheviot Hills
OS 1:50 000 Landranger Sheet 80

Start/Finish: West Wood car park, GR 926049, 1/2 mile (0.8km) W from Harbottle.

Distance: 4 3/4 miles (7.6km)

Height Gain: 581ft (177m)

Grade: 2

Walking Time: 2 1/2-3 hours

Accommodation & Parking:
A choice of accommodation in Rothbury, with a limited selection in Harbottle and surrounds. Parking at West Wood Forest Enterprise car park

Let Alone; Let Alone!
Or'all droon Harbottle,
An the Peels
An' the bonny Hallystone.

Anon.

The Route: The car park at West Wood provides a quiet start for this exciting walk as the track rises south-west to a wicket gate opening onto the heathery fell. *Although there is an MOD red flag at the gateway it only applies to the area S and W beyond the moorland fence.* Once through the gate veer right, i.e. west with the ascending track to

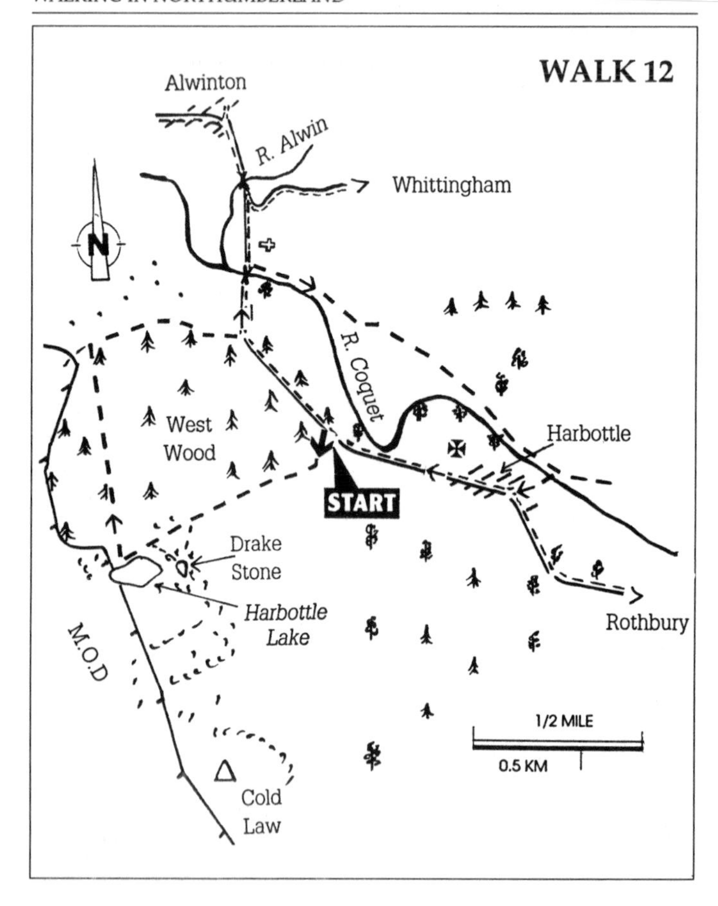

Harbottle Hills. Folding fells ripple to the rock strewn skyline, crowned by the now visible Drake Stone (1), as the silver birch and rowan flanked route rises parallel to the perimeter of coniferous West Wood.

As height is gained swing left, at a post-marked fork, onto a stony peat path winding through deep heather, rising to the awesome block of sculptured fell sandstone. There is no mistaking the Drake

Stone, standing head and shoulders above the surrounding earthfast rocks known locally as the Duck Stones. Fine vistas of Coquetdale present themselves east and south, with the sooty waters of Harbottle Lough (2) immediately west.

From the Drake Stone rejoin the track west, and at a lakeside mire veer right via two waymarked stiles onto a posted shoreline path west. To the right note the burnt heather fells littered with dozens of partially finished or faulted millstones (3), many clearly visible from the path. Continue with the north shore of this gull-favoured lough as far as the boundary fence and warning notices of the MOD ranges. Not wishing to enter this shell shattered land, which has little to excite the walker, turn right and follow a fenceside trod north to enter West Wood.

Although not marked on the OS map as a path *(the map shows a parallel public path through MOD land to the west)* this pleasing 3/4 mile (1.2km) trek through West Wood is assisted by intermittent fence posts. Crags and forest clearings en route ensure visual variation prior to the wicket gate exit, at the wood's northern perimeter, which leads onto the cart track known as The Swire (4). Once on this gated track, with its MOD signs and fine views of Barrow Hill west

Old millstones by Harbottle Lough

and a spread of Coquetdale east, turn right through the fieldgate and descend to the valley road above Alwinton Bridge.

The road is followed north for 300yds/m to cross the River Coquet by Alwinton Bridge before turning right, below Low Alwinton and Alwinton Church (5), onto the bridleway known as the Border County Ride. Surfaced to Park House, a pleasing stone structure, then a cart track beyond, with fine sightings of the Drake Stone, it traverses the pastures between Hob's Knowe, Camp Knowes (6) and the crumbling remains of Harbottle Castle (7) for just over a mile to the footbridge and ford leading to Harbottle. A village of character and historic pedigree Harbottle leads the walker west with the road for the final 1/2 mile (0.8km) roadside return to West Wood car park.

ITEMS OF INTEREST ALONG THE WAY

(1) THE DRAKE, or DRAAG, STONE. Northumberland's largest single outcrop of fell sandstone, standing some 30ft (9m) high and weighing in excess of 2000 tons, tops the ridge of Harbottle Crag. In profile it presents the lines of an Elizabethan galleon; blunt at the northern end and sharp at the south (the result of Ice Age abrasion). Could this profile have produced the name of 'Drake Stone'? As with many other Northumbrian features the Drake Stone is said to possess magical healing powers; sick children were hauled over its huge bulk by ropes - if they survived it was due to the Stone's curative powers!

(2) HARBOTTLE LOUGH. A dark, brooding tarn, whose hypothermic waters are said to induce instant demise to swimmers. Centuries ago there were plans afoot to drain the lough, plans that were abandoned when the workmen fled after hearing a stentorian voice boom forth from the dark waters, a 'Let Alone, Let Alone,' warning.

(3) MILLSTONES. In great quantities these millstones were fashioned in the last century from the sandstones of Harbottle Crags. Rejected and discarded stones, the majority 5ft (1.52m) in diameter and with a circular or square central hole, can be seen surrounding Harbottle Lough and the Drake Stone.

(4) THE SWIRE. Old spelling 'Swyre', an Anglo-Saxon word meaning a neck of land or col, on the ancient route from Redesdale to

Coquetdale.

(5) ALWINTON CHURCH. Of unusual construction, due to the sloping ground, the twelfth century chancel stands thirteen steps above the altar and ten above the nave.

(6) CAMP KNOWES. The campsite of the besieging Scots in the thirteenth century during a vain attempt to capture Harbottle Castle. Canonballs recovered between the knowes and the castle confirm this military presence.

(7) HARBOTTLE CASTLE. *Mary Queen of Scots did NOT sleep here, but her mother-in-law did.* Little has remained of this twelfth century castle since the 1600s. Partially destroyed following Bannockburn, it was restored in 1515 to allow Margaret Tudor (wife of the Earl of Angus, sister of Henry VIII and widow of James IV of Scotland) sanctuary for the birth of her daughter. A daughter who became the mother-in-law of the ill-fated Mary Queen of Scots and grandmother of James I of England and VI of Scotland.

Walk 13: A Holy Place and a Magic Place
HOLYSTONE, LADY'S WELL and DOVE CRAG

Type of Walk: *Although Lady's Well, a tranquil place set in open country, is visited initially the bulk of the walk is unashamedly through Holystone Forest to the Fairy Glen and Lanternside Cleugh. Never overpowering and with extensive sightings of distant fells, it passes by oak, beech, silver birch and conifer and is home to a wide variety of active wildlife. The paths/tracks traversing relatively level ground are well waymarked; we utilise the green and red arrowheads for this circuit.*

Maps: OS 1:50 000 Landranger Sheet 80 & 81

Start/Finish: Forest Enterprise Holystone Forest car park/picnic area, GR 949023, 1/2 mile (0.8km) WSW of Holystone village; which is 9 miles (14.4km) W from Rothbury.

Distance: 5 miles (8km)

Height Gain: 492ft (150m)

Grade: 2

Walking Time: 3 hours

Accommodation & Parking:
Limited village and farmhouse B/Bs, wider range in Rothbury. Free parking in Forest Enterprise Holystone car park and picnic area.

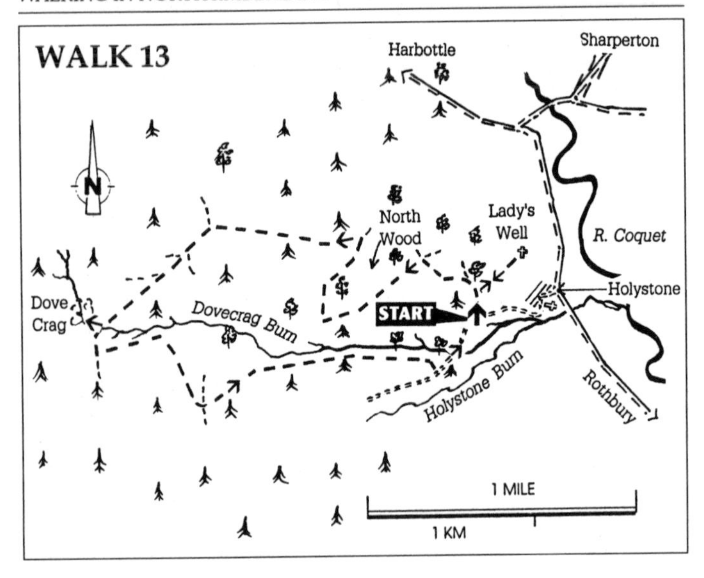

The Route: From the car park/picnic area walk north with the forest track, turning right onto a prepared path (green marker and finger post 'Lady's Well') 100yds/m beyond the kissing gate, marked with the green, orange and red waymarks. Pass through the dark conifers to cross an open pasture, above the pleasing village of Holystone, to the sylvan surrounds of Lady's Well (1) and the statue dedicated to St Paulinus (2). Return on the outward path to the forest track.

Turn right on this red and orange way as it sweeps left, prior to entering the trees, left, on a needle strewn pathway rising west and north-west between the forest's edge and Campville's pastures to the crosstracks above the field corner. Veer left with the red marker onto a splendid section; gnarled, contorted oak of North Wood (3) on the right and glorious vistas south-east extending over Coquet's horseshoes at Hepple, to the unmistakable fells/crags of Tosson Hill, Ravens Heugh and Simonside. At the southern corner of North Wood, by a well placed wooden seat, turn right (red marker) and rise with the copper-carpeted track alongside a line of venerable beech trees.

As this colourful tree-line is left behind the red markers guide us through conifer, with the path almost doubling back on itself, onto the kilometre long, grassy path west through Turnberry. This is a straight way that eventually emerges, with a fine viewpoint north to Hedgehope and Muckle Cheviot, onto a main haul road running north-south. Clamber left onto this wide forest road and follow it south, with our faithful red markers, for 1/4 mile (0.4km) to a road junction. Here the road is abandoned for a smaller waymarked forest track to the right, i.e. south-west, a route that is shared with a public footpath for some of its journey of 600yds/m, to the diversion leading right to the picturesque and unexpected sandstone outcrops and waterfall of Dove Crag (4).

Return from this Fairy Glen, veering south and crossing the public footpath east, to walk below the heathery banking of Sandy's Sike; eventually to swing right at the marked fork. The way continues through bird filled conifers, where drilling woodpeckers and chirping finches abound. Cross another marked public footpath north-east. A track and pathway now dance east along the rim of Lanternside Cleugh above winding Dovecrag Burn, home to moisture loving ferns, liverworts and many mosses.

Leave the cleugh by swinging right, i.e. south to emerge onto the MOD road that runs through Holystone Nature Reserve and the extensive and visible earthworks (5). For those interested a short diversion right is recommended. The descending tarmac left, i.e. east, on the course of a Roman Road (6), soon returns the walker to journey's end at the picnic area/car park.

ITEMS OF INTEREST ALONG THE WAY

(1) LADY'S WELL. This holy well, a spring of pure bright water with a central cross and adjoining statue of St Paulinus, stands within a small copse. The spring even to this day supplies nearby Holystone with water, praised in the last century by Stephen Oliver as 'the best water in the country for mixing with spirit'. In the fifth century Lady's Well was associated with St Ninian, apostle to the Border country, and in the twelfth century a priory for Augustinian nuns was erected nearby.

(2) ST PAULINUS. A Roman missionary who baptized some 3000 Northumbrians, in AD 627, in the clear waters of Lady's Well. Busy

Paulinus also baptized thousands in 36 days in the River Glen (Walk 1), only 17 miles (27.2km) due north. The stone statue was brought from Alnwick in 1780.

(3) NORTH WOOD. This ancient coppiced oak wood, seldom seen in Northumberland, produced charcoal for iron smelting. A practice that ceased with the advent of coke.

(4) DOVE CRAG. Known locally as 'Fairy Glen', and reputed to be home to the little people, it is a magic place, a pencil thin waterfall dropping into a hollowed basin and surrounded by rounded and tree-framed sandstone outcrops.

(5) CROSS DYKES. Road blocks, ditches and earthworks across the course of a Roman Road as it clears the forest at GR 947022. Difficult to date, this particular control was probably built in the 1500s to slow down Reiver incursions from the north and west. A local order was issued in 1561 for 'great trenches and ditches' to be dug.

(6) ROMAN ROAD. This section ran from 'Bremnium' (Rochester on the A68) to the cross-county road, known as the Devil's Causeway, leading north to cross the Tweed at West Ord.

Walk 14: *'Festina Lente'* - Hasten Gently

SIMONSIDE FOREST - RAVENS HEUGH - SIMONSIDE CRAGS - DOVE CRAG

Type of Walk: *This forest and fell adventure lays to rest the myth that forest walks and 'green tunnels' are synonymous. The waymarked route, embracing the great crags of Simonside and its satellites, is varied, scenic, challenging and vastly rewarding. As this hill walker's Mecca attracts many devotees during summer weekends, I would suggest crisp, far-seeing winter days to savour Simonside and solitude.*

Maps: OS 1:25 000 Pathfinder, 500 & 511
OS 1:50 000 Landranger Sheet 81, Alnwick & Morpeth

Start/Finish: Simonside Forest car park, GR 037996, 1 3/4 miles (2.8km) SW, via Great Tosson, from Rothbury.

Distance: 6 3/4 miles (10.8km)

Height Gain: 985ft (300m)

Grade: 3, due to two steep ascents; 4 if scrambling on Old Stell Crag and its un-named neighbour.

Walking Time: $3^{1}/_{2}$-4 hours

Accommodation & Parking:
A range of accommodation available in Rothbury, with surrounding farmhouse B/Bs. Free parking - Simonside Forest car park/picnic area.

The Route: From the car park, with its map and information board, walk west with the green, orange and red waymarks. An ordinary start to an extraordinary journey, and as the winding road gradually ascends look out for woodpeckers and finches in the lodgepole pine fringes. After 600yds/m the green route departs left; we continue west for $^{1}/_{2}$ mile (0.8km) to a waymarked fork, where outward orange/red markers direct left. Ignore them and carry on ahead, i.e. west, on what is the return orange route. Our guides are now marker posts, with orange arrowheads on the reverse side.

The forest road descends to a newly fenced lay-by; veer sharp left for a stimulating hike south-south-west, revealing the delights of Coquetdale to the Cheviot Hills beyond. As Chesterhope Burn is crossed the track swings right, rising for 433yds (400m) to a reverse marker post on the right-hand verge. At this point turn sharp left, hopping up a clay path onto a coppery carpet through the filtered light of Chesterhope Beeches (1).

A steep rise south-west, past reverse waymarks, leads from the

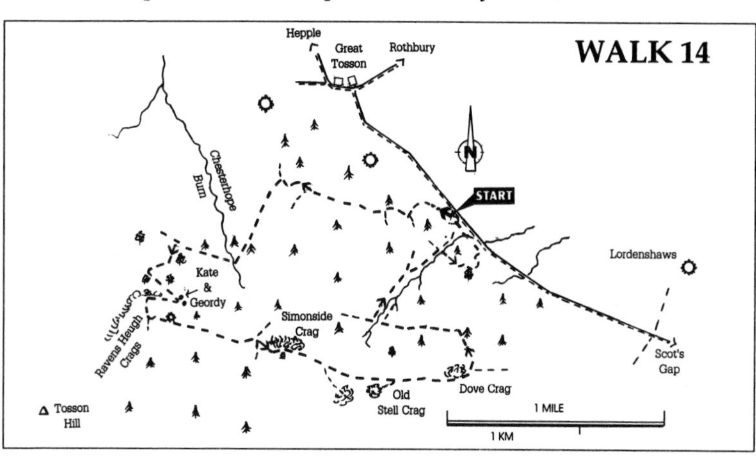

beech wood into a mongrel stand of silver birch, oak, rowan - some coppiced - and a variety of pines. Never dull, the slithery zigzag squirms roughly south, climbing a root-strewn way that squeezes between trees and a gallery of sculptured sandstones. The most bizarre are the mushroom styled pair known as 'Kate & Geordy', reminiscent of the Pepper-Pot Bride Stones on the North York Moors, heralding the onset of heather fells and Ravens Heugh crags. Enjoy the inspiring vistas in the northern quarter from these grandstands, over the noisy bird sanctuary of Caistron, the humps of Hedgehope and Cheviot and west to Catcleuch Shin.

At Ravens Heugh's forest perimeter turn left on swiped heather rising to the notice 'Orange Walk Return'; at this point descend left, i.e. east/south-east with the forest track for the great crags of Simonside. Arriving at the junction below the naked rock leave the reverse orange-markers by turning right and immediately left, off the road, with the red waymarks. Here a peat and stone trod makes a direct ascending assault, of 165ft (50m), to the cairned cist on Simonside summit (2). Ravens Heugh was good, Simonside is better.

Leave east with the red markers, on a peaty track through heather and tussock where two rocky crags, one cairned but unnamed, the other called Old Stell Crag, invite inspection by means of thin heathery trods. The choice is yours, but heed well the placement of your feet when exploring the rocky crags. The main red-marked fellway, home to red grouse and the seldom seen blackcock, carries on descending east-south-east just north of the crags, and is joined later by Old Stell Crag's trod prior to Dove Crag ahead. Sightings of the North Sea at Druridge Bay precede our departure from 'Cragland' as the way veers left at the notice 'Red Walk Return'. Note the long path east to Lordenshaws (3) for another day.

Continue north into tight conifers leading to a forest track. Once on the track follow it west as it inclines to join a haul road north, i.e. right with the red markers. 400yds/m on this descending dirt road brings us to a red marker directing right onto a mud and root-ridden path, dropping through lodgepole pine parallel to and above Coe Burn.

At the waymarked crosspaths below, leave the red route to join the green way, travelling right and crossing Coe Burn by the wooden footbridge. This short stroll, punctuated with frequent markers, loops east/north/west by track and trod through open tree cover, paddling to the picnic area and the adjacent car park. A non-taxing stretch in which the hordes of seasonal crossbills can be seen and enjoyed.

ITEMS OF INTEREST ALONG THE WAY

(1) CHESTERHOPE BEECHES. The remains of a larger beech wood, planted in and around the 1870s, by the first Baron Armstong of Cragside. W.G. Armstrong was the founder of W.G. Armstrong & Co, original inventor and manufacturer of hydraulic machinery for use in northern lead mines, which later developed into the massive armaments empire that became Vickers Armstrong of Tyneside. After acquiring nearby Cragside, Lord Armstrong produced hydro-electricity and made the house the first in the world to be lit by electricity.

(2) SIMONSIDE CRAGS, 1409ft (430m). A classic example of inward facing escarpments and outward folding flanks produced by strata tilt within the great crescent of Fell Sandstone, laid down in the Carboniferous era, south of the Cheviot Hills. Escarpments that provide not only far-reaching views, but are also the eye-catching fulcrum of Northumberland, seen from every corner of the county. They are also a bit of a honey-pot for the northern rock climber (first recorded in 1902).

(3) LORDENSHAWS. Towards the site of the nearby prehistoric hillfort on Garleigh Moor, via the path leading from Lordenshaws car park, there stand two earthfast boulders exhibiting 'Cup and Ring' marks. These grooved concentric rings surrounding sunken cup marks are also found on out-standing boulders on Weetwood Moor and Doddington Moor by Wooler; also Roughting Linn above Ford. They date back to the Bronze Age and are thought to have religious significance concerning life and death as they are also seen on standing stones and cists.

Walk15: The Kielder Stane - With Feral Goats and Curlews

KIELDER CASTLE, DEADWATER, PEEL FELL AND PEDEN'S CAVE

Type of Walk: *An energetic circular hill walk for those who relish 'putting themselves about a bit', over purple heather and bent-clad fells to the charismatic Kielder Stane. A journey by redundant rail-bed, forest track and airy peaty fells revealing two countries, two seas, a Covenanter's cave and a gigantic Border post box. Crossing wild and lonely uplands, home to a wide spectrum of wildlife, so please ensure the status quo by keeping to the paths and tracks.*

Maps: OS 1:25 000 Explorer 1, Kielder Water
OS 1:50 000 Landranger Sheet 80, The Cheviot Hills

Start/Finish: Kielder Castle Visitor Centre, GR 633935, 10 miles (16km) NW from Kielder Water dam.

Distance: 12½ miles (20km)

Height Gain: 2065ft (630m)

Grade: 3 or 4 - depending on weather conditions / visibility. The way is marked with green posts bearing Forest Enterprise yellow arrowheads; albeit on the reverse side.

Walking Time: 7 hours

Accommodation & Parking:
Limited to Kielder village, surrounding B/Bs and camp/caravan site. Extensive parking in Kielder Castle Wood car park - pay.

On Kielder-side the wind blaws wide;
There sounds nae hunting horn
That rings sae sweet as the winds that beat
Round the banks where Tyne was born.

A.C. Swinburne, *A Jacobite's Exile*

The Route: Leave the Visitor Centre with eager anticipation, swinging left at the small roundabout to cross the River North Tyne, then right through Kielder village, via Castle Drive, to cross the main road into a small snickert at the north end of the houses. Turn right by the garages, onto what was the rail-bed of the North British Railway (1), following it north-west for 2¾ miles (4.4km).

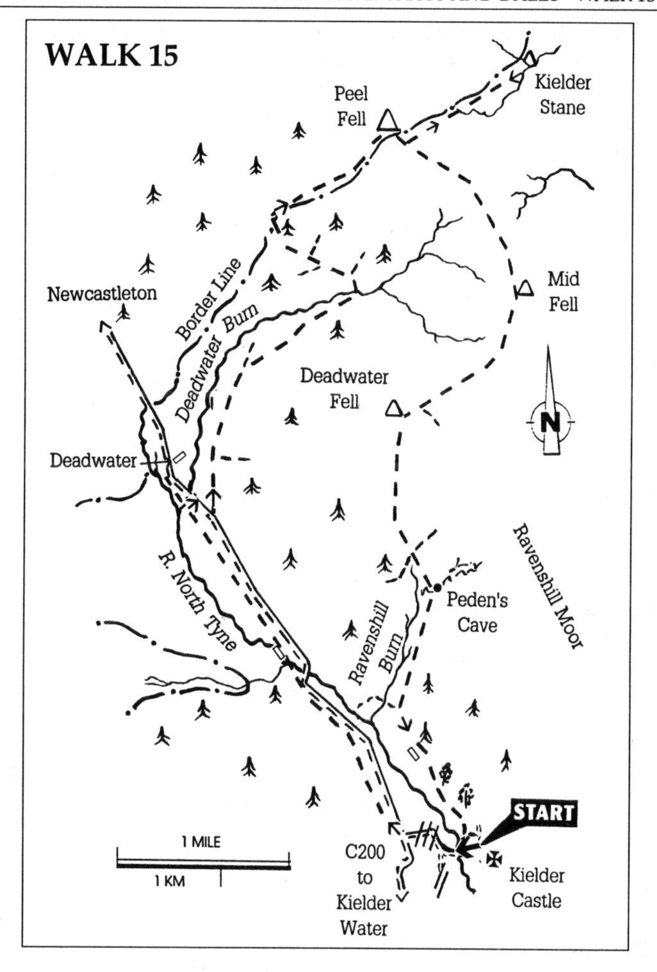

This easy section follows the course of the River North Tyne, past the old sawmill, Bellsburnfoot Cottage and Bell's Moor. Of interest are the limekilns seen on Bell's Moor. Fired by local coal they provided 'lime' from local limestone needed to sweeten the surrounding acid moorland. As Deadwater Farm (2) approaches leave the old track at the twin-arched bridge by turning sharp right through the conifer strip by Deadwater Burn (2), to the main road. Turn right at the green marker for a short vergeside walk to the next forest road junction, marked with a Forest Enterprise 'Walkers Welcome' sign.

Turn sharp left, i.e. north between conifer and cleared ground and at the first fork continue north via the gated left-hand track contouring above the gouged gully of Deadwater Burn. Ignore further incoming forest tracks, one left and one right, as the now airy track descends to cross Deadwater Burn. The dark-hued bulk of Peel Fell dominates as the forest track ascends due north-west before coming to an abrupt halt at the tree bound grassy turning circle. Continue right into a ride on a narrow tussock-clad trod, walking north for 130 paces to the broken drystone wall and forest fence at Rushy Knowe, GR 614989.

Pass through the fence/wall turning right for a steep plod north-east, out of the conifers, to rise 762ft (232m) over the next half-mile or so alongside the border fence, bound for the stones and hags of Peel Fell's summit. The terrain is ideal for feral goats (3), and at the summit rim are two rounded posts and a tidy cairn to the left. Once over the rim veer half right to thread south-east, with the occasional post, through Peel Fell's stygian peat hags to the crumbling, grass covered summit cairn (4). Continue south-east, descending with the border fence for 250yds/m to the prominent strainer post that angles the border line left, i.e. north-east.

At this point, which is in fact the continuing Border Line between Northumberland and Scotland, descend left for 3/4 mile (1.2km) with peaty path and fence approaching Kielderstone Cleugh. And as Wylies Sike trickles into the cleugh there suddenly appears, all 1500 tons of it, the Kielder Stane (5), grass-capped and riding high in a sea of purple heather. After inspection return to the strainer post below Peel Fell ridge.

From here turn left, to rise and fall south and south-west, over the crescent rim of Deadwater Corrie by Mid Fell and Deadwater Moor, to the coned summit of Deadwater Fell. At first glance a desert of peat and heather, however, aided by rotting and broken metal/wood posts it can be traversed safely, even in poor visibility. First, south-east from post to post, between the bearings of 113° to

Kielder Castle

195° magnetic to Mid Fell's cairned bump (6); beyond, the posts are more frequent and a bearing of 215° magnetic leads past the dark tarn lurking on Deadwater col. Here a new road assists passage to the electronic mish-mash of Deadwater Fell's summit. Fine views south of the jinking dale of the North Tyne are revealed and hopefully a glimpse of the resident herd of feral goats (3) also.

Beyond the masts, assorted buildings and fell sandstone crags follow the wide track, descending south, for 580yds (500m) between Ravenshill Moor and the forest fringes. Prior to the track swinging right into the forest, pass left onto open moorland, GR 628959, and follow the fence on your right hand south as far as the first electric pole. Veer left through the tangle of heather to the pole, then drop right over a line of serrated crags; at the centre of these a stunted tree clings despairingly to a wind-worn overhang in the immediate vicinity of Peden's Cave (7). Leaving the tiny cave, cross Ravenshill Moor, seasonal home to whaup and peewit, on faint sheep traces south past a crumbling sheep stell above and east of Ravenshill Burn. Ahead the forest fence stile, GR 628952, allows passage into a replanted stand, then via a rutted track swing south to join a major forest road.

Follow this wide road south-east above Ravenshill Farm, between thinned stands of mature conifers, and as it winds left past a walled pasture, join the waymarked Duke's Drive pathway through the beech trees to Castle Wood car park and journey's end at Kielder Castle Visitor Centre.

ITEMS OF INTEREST ALONG THE WAY

(1) NORTH BRITISH RAILWAY. Known locally as the 'Counties Line', it was North Tynedale's lifeline from 1826, carrying goods/ provisions up-line and coal/coffins down-line. Pulled for many years by the Dipper, the ill-fated engine involved in the Tay Bridge tragedy, which was sent to the 'Counties Line' as no Scots driver would cross its footplate. The line closed in 1958, after 96 years of service.

(2) DEADWATER - FARM and BURN. Farmed in the mid 1600s by Janet Hann, who made a living from agriculture and also from 'resetting'. A Resetter or Fence traded in and disposed of reived (stolen) livestock. A few hundred yards north, from Deadwater Farm, water seeps into Liddel Water, eventually running into the Irish Sea. Nearby Deadwater Burn, later the North Tyne, flows to the North Sea.

(3) FERAL GOATS. Two small herds of semi-wild goats, up to twenty per group, can be seen around the forest fringes and craggy upper slopes of Peel Fell and Deadwater Fell. Their numbers are kept low by a combination of poor feeding and severe winters. The 'billies' display distinct sweeping horns and the 'nannies' give birth to their 'kids' in early spring.

(4) PEEL FELL, 1975ft (602m). Dark, sombre and oft capped in cloud this Cheviot hill provides, it is said, sightings of the Irish Sea and the North Sea. I have seen both, but never on the same day. Lakeland peaks Skiddaw and Blencathra are frequently visible.

(5) THE KIELDER STONE. A 1500 ton, 39,000 cubic feet block of Carboniferous fell sandstone, laid down some 280 million years ago and later pummelled and pressured into the outcrops and crags visible today. By a strange coincidence this gargantuan rock straddles the Border Line and during the Border Wars was used as a depository

or post box for cross-border mail. The Kielder Stane (local pronunciation) carries the letters 'N & D' (the D in reverse, perhaps the work of an illiterate stonemason). Such marks indicate the English boundaries of the Dukes of Northumberland and the Scottish boundaries of the Earls of Douglas and are seen on many man-made boundary stones. Nearby Kielderhead Moor is a designated SSSI particularly sensitive from March to July.

(6) MID FELL. An untidy tumulus, the burial site of Iron Age chieftains, marks its summit dome, standing above the fine corrie of Deadwater.

(7) PEDEN'S CAVE. In this cramped, damp hole Sandy (Alexander) Peden, a Covenanting preacher from Hawick, is said to have sheltered in the seventeenth century to avoid capture. On Rubers Law, by Denholm, stands 'Peden's Pulpit', and to the east a huge cairn caps Padon (anglicised spelling) Hill. Sandy was eventually captured and sentenced to life imprisonment on Bass Rock in the Firth of Forth.

Walk 16: A Marathon Walk
THE CIRCUMNAMBULATION of KIELDER WATER

In somer, when the shaws be sheen
And leves be large and long.
Stephen Oliver, *Rambles in Northumberland*

Type of Walk: *26 miles (41.6km) at one go is, by any standards, a weighty and continuous challenge that demands respect. Although described in full it can be done in stages, returning by means of the Kielder Water ferry Osprey; or shorter circular walks can be enjoyed by utilising sections such as Bull Crag, The Belling or Bakethin and Kielder Viaduct. This serious but scenic marathon that can be treated as a Challenge Walk by those who wish little reward save that of personal satisfaction. Or an extended experience for those who wish to share the unique habitat of forest and water with the resident wildlife and the memories of the past. The way is by forest and waterside paths and tracks, some prepared, some not, adequately waymarked with 'Otterprint' symbols, and for the challenge walkers contains twelve checkpoints to be recorded.*

If the entire circuit is to be tackled it is advisable to secure the Kielder Water Circuit Challenge Walk pack, from Tower Knowe Visitor Centre or Leaplish Waterside Park, which provides, for a small fee, walk details, map, checkpoint card and pen. If walking alone always leave details of your route with others.

Maps: OS 1:25 000 Explorer 1, Kielder Water
OS 1:50 000 Landranger Sheet 80, The Cheviot Hills

Start/Finish: Leaplish Lodge, GR 660878, on the S shore of Kielder Water reservoir; $5^{1}/_{2}$ miles (8.8km) W from Falstone and $5^{3}/_{4}$ miles (9.2km) SSE of Kielder. At Leaplish Lodge the challenge walker can 'clock in/out'. Shortened sections start at Bull Crag, Tower Knowe, Hawkhope, Bakethin or Hawkhirst.

Distance: 26 miles (41.6km)

Height Gain: 600ft (183m)

Grade: 4

Walking Time: 10-12 hours

Accommodation & Parking:
Limited accommodation at Falstone and Leaplish Waterside Park, B/B and caravan/campsite at Kielder and surrounds. Car parks at Leaplish Park.

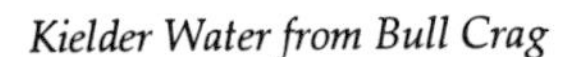

Kielder Water from Bull Crag

The Route: The formalities of 'clocking in' over, leave Leaplish Lodge car park with the 'Shoreline Footpath', a way, by Leaplish Sike and avenues of stately, two and a half centuries old beech, that leads east to Checkpoint 1. Continue with the shoreline path, by Kielder Water-Ski club, making for the bulky promontory of Bull Crag as the grass trod ascends to Otterstone viewpoint (1).

Now on Bull Crag the waymarks direct east onto the remains of the old North Tyne Road (today most lies beneath the water) prior to reaching Checkpoint 2. Ahead, over the water, the dam appears but a mile or so away, by foot it's more than six as we leave the picnic site by a sandy track west. Look and listen, for this area is favoured by the secretive goshawk; also for the Otterprint waymark leading west into the trees and the C200 road over Cranecleugh Bridge. Once over the bridge veer left by Cranecleugh Burn, and with waymarks on the right stumble over tussocks to the jetties and clubhouse of Whickhope Anchorage. Beyond lies the viewpoint of

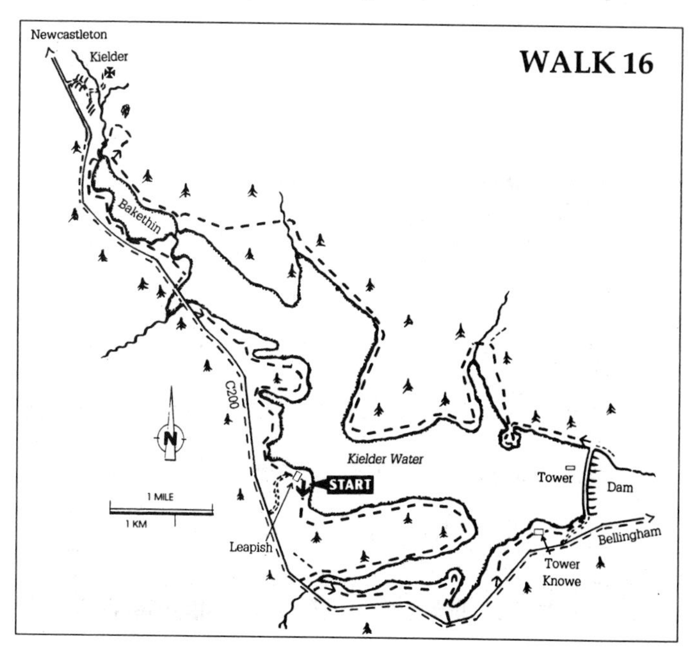

Merlin Brae (2) and Checkpoint 3.

Carry on west with the shore, passing Little Whickhope water-ski school, to emerge onto the tarmac of the C200. Bear left for a dull 3/4 mile (1.2km) of roadside walking before nipping left into scrub on a distinct waymarked path that winds to Northumbrian Water's often busy Tower Knowe Visitor Centre (refreshments if required). Use the minute humpback bridge to escape north to a heather, cairn and plaque (3) clad headland bearing Checkpoint 4. The massive dam (4) now dominates and can be crossed north, with ease and not a little awe, to Hawkhirst car park/picnic place (4).

More Otterprint waymarks mark the route to the Belling peninsula, one of the most pleasing and interesting stretches along the 10 mile (16km) north shore. Although through a mix of trees, this root strewn path is never far from the sights and sounds of the water as it reaches the land-strand anchoring the picturesque Belling peninsula, home to Checkpoint 5 and spectacular quarry cliffs.

Return to the 'mainland' and swing left, i.e. north-north-west joining the North Haul forest road, and at GR 693893 search for a waymark on the left directing us into the conifers and dropping north-west to the footbridge spanning the inlet of Belling Burn, GR 660913. Once over turn left, following the distinct trod snaking south, to Cock Stoor peninsula and Checkpoint 6. The tortuous way, in complete isolation, continues to and around the never ending headland of Wind Hill to Plashetts Quarry (5) and Checkpoint 7. Follow the Otterprints north to Checkpoint 8 and Plashetts Incline (5), to eventually emerge onto the forest road at GR 660913.

The forest road is our guide for the next 2 miles (3.2km), taking us past Gowanburn and Bakethin Weir; then with the waymark descend south to join the now grassed over north-west rail-bed of the redundant Border Counties Line (6), a fine walkway which leads to Kielder Viaduct (6). Here we leave it right via a stepped path to reach Checkpoint 9, and later a tarmac road, dropping north and west via Butteryhaugh Bridge to Bakethin car park by the Counties Line rail-bed. Rejoin the line walking north-west for a short distance until the rail-bed peters out; here pass by narrow pathway and off-set fence onto a minor road.

Immediately turn left at the metal gate and accompanying Otterprint waymark for a delightful section through mature, thinned conifer stands close by the shores of Bakethin reservoir. Waymarks abound along the tarmac and hard core tracks and thin woodland trods through this environmentally sensitive area. A short detour to the well equipped bird hide overlooking Bakethin and the Skew-Arched viaduct is well worth a visit. All too soon our route returns to the C200 road from where a left turn at the Bakethin Weir sign leads once more to the waterside.

After the 22 mile (32.5km) mark veer left then right to Checkpoint 10 leading to Lewis Burn Bridge over the C200 road. Once over bear left, signposted Matthews Linn car park, as the path ploughs through shoulder high willow herb (in late summer) and midge infested scrub to Hawkhirst peninsula and the penultimate Checkpoint 11. At the southern tip of Hawkhirst Checkpoint 12 appears but a few hundred yards over the water; unfortunately the winding waterside path has a further mile to travel, west and south-east, before finally clocking-in at Leaplish Lodge, at the end of a truly memorable trek.

It remains the right of Northumbrian Water, in the interests of the walker, to make any minor route changes they consider necessary.

ITEMS OF INTEREST ALONG THE WAY

(1) JUBILEE PLANTATION, circa 1977, commemorates Queen Elizabeth's Silver Jubilee with a scatter of Scots pine and stone cromlechs and offers superb views over Kielder Water to the coned Deadwater Fell.

(2) INFORMATION PANEL describing deer and red squirrel and identifying Merlin Brae, Elf Kirk, Tower Knowe and the Dam.

(3) COMMEMORATION PLAQUE for the 1976 Kielder Water Scheme, and alongside details of a third century settlement.

(4) KIELDER WATER DAM, site of an axe murder most foul in the 1300s and today site of a dam holding back 44,000 million gallons of water by means of 5.3 million cubic feet of puddle clay, stone and concrete 1250yds (1154m) long.

(5) PLASHETTS - COLLIERY, INCLINE and QUARRY. The coal mine opened in 1773, coal later being transported by 'inclined' wagon-track to a depot on the now immersed 'Counties Line'. Annual production of coal increased to 100,000 tons in 1911 causing heavy pollution in the area, which resulted in lawsuits, by local

farmers, for loss of crops and animals. The quarry was the main source of whinstone for the dam. The area is rich in fell, forest and water wildlife.

(6) BORDER COUNTIES RAILWAY and 'SKEW-ARCHED' VIADUCT. A lifeline for North Tyne Dale, the railway operated from Bellingham, via Riccarton Junction to Newcastleton and Hawick, from 1862 to 1958. It ran over the spectacular Kielder Viaduct circa 1862, known as the 'Skew-Arched' bridge on account of its angled arches and off-set pillars designed to withstand the seasonal surges of the once violent River North Tyne.

Walk 17: Blood and Thunder

SIDWOOD, BLACK MIDDENS, BOG HEAD and WOODHOUSE

Type of Walk: *A figure of eight journey, on both sides of tinkling Tarset Burn, that provides a shorter walk if desired. For the student of Border Wars and the Reiving Times this walk is a must, as it is for those who delight in the flora and fauna of forest, burnside and fellside fringes. Waymarked for its entirety on distinct paths and country lanes this ramble is of interest every step of the way.*

Maps: OS 1:25 000 Explorer 1, Kielder Water
OS 1:50 000 Landranger Sheet 80, The Cheviot Hills

Start/Finish: Forest Enterprise Sidwood car park and picnic area, GR 776891, 6 miles (9.6km) north-west from Bellingham, via a narrow signposted lane beyond Greenhaugh.

Distance: 4 miles (6.4km)

Height Gain: 197ft (60m)

Grade: 2

Walking Time: 2-2½ hours

Accommodation & Parking:
Village inn B/B in Greenhaugh, wider range available in Bellingham. Parking etc. at Sidwood car park, GR 776891.

The Route: Leave the car park and wooded glade picnic area, walking north-west with the wide forest road to beyond the washed walls of Sidwood Cottage; here turn right onto a waymarked ('Reiver's Way') path. A sylvan journey through rhododendron to

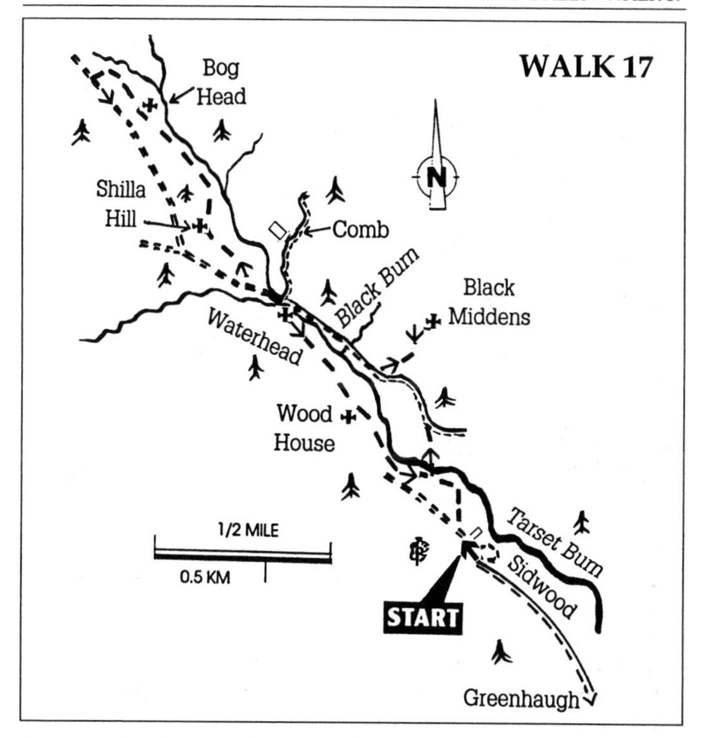

the birch-lined Tarset Burn, said to be haunted by horse drawn chariots at midnight, is then followed left along its true right bank, by gated path to a footbridge. Veering right, cross the burn and with a marked pasture path walk north to a U bend in the country lane ahead. Continue north-west with the lane to Black Middens car park.

Turn right through the swing-gate, ascending with a winding pasture track to the partially restored bastle of Black Middens (1). After inspection and pleasing views of the Tarset valley return to the car park and lane, veering right to cross Black Burn, either by roadbridge, ford or footbridge. Beyond, after a short section of lane, Tarset Burn is crossed by bridge above Waterhead, and with the ascending waymarked lane rise to a further marker, on the right,

Black Midden's Bastle

leading onto a grass path.

This winding way by a stand of young spruce rises to the ruins of Starr Head Bastle (2) - crumbling stones surrounding struggling rowan - on Shilla Hill. The pathway carries on north, easing down through mature conifer to the beech and birch lined banks of Tarset. Wind north-west with the burn bank for just over half a mile to the ruins of Corbie Castle at Bog Head, home to reiver and folk hero, Bartholomew Milburn. Hence the castles more popular name - 'Barty's Pele (3).

Leave the pele to pass the remains of a Long House (4) on the edge of a poorly, if at all, drained haugh; then rise to the marked forest road. Turn left, descending and forking left at the two junctions, to reach Waterhead (5). The cottage, with original bastle cornerstones built into its surrounding wall, is passed by crossing Blacklinn Burn footbridge onto a marked path leading south-south-east to Wood House Bastle (6). Keep a good look out, on your right hand, for this grassed-over ruin - it's easily missed - prior to arriving back at the first footbridge of our outward journey.

The final leg to Sidwood car park is with the outward path, equally appealing, if not more so, in reverse.

ITEMS OF INTEREST ALONG THE WAY

(1) BLACK MIDDENS. More than a bastle, but not quite a pele tower, this restored structure and the later cottage close by, illustrate the protection needed to exist in the harsh times and environment of North Tyne Dale.

(2) STARR HEAD BASTLE. The highest of the bastles, sighted on Shilla Hill, Starr Head was the look-out for Reiver incursion from Liddesdale. In the late seventeenth century it was home to Corbett Jack, friend and ally of Barty Milburn of Corbies Castle.

(3) BARTY'S PELE. Towards the end of the seventeenth century, Scots reivers came to Bog Head by Tarset Burn, making off with Bartholomew's sheep. Not a man to take such villany lying down, Barty and Corbett Jack set off on a 'hot trod' over the Border. His sheep however could not be found, therefore in accordance with 'hot trod' traditions Barty subsituted his lost sheep with a Scot's flock. A chase in reverse resulted in wounds for Barty and death for Corbett Jack and two Scots. This Border skirmish was recorded with Barty's fatal words: 'his heid spang alang the heather like an onion'!

(4) LONG HOUSE. One of many to be found on the surrounds of the North Tyne valley, erected in the eighteenth century when relative peace settled on the inhabitants of the border counties. Long low buildings, with a single door, in which stock and farmer lived albeit in separate rooms.

(5) WATERHEAD. A seventeeth century bastle that survived, and was occupied well into the nineteenth century, although plagued by Liddesdale Armstrongs as recorded by J. Hunter of Waterhead: 'They ran a daytime foray, raysing fire and driving many nolt, sheep and goats away'.

(6) WOOD HOUSE BASTLE. Basically a fortified farmhouse, with walls of great thickness, one door, tiny windows and a thatched roof. In vogue in the sixteenth and seventeenth centuries they can be found throughout the border fringes.

Walk 18: Wallington Estate Walk

FALLOWLEES NATURE RESERVE, FONTBURN RESERVOIR TO GREENLEIGHTON HILL

Type of Walk: *A circular journey, in the heart of Northumberland, from the now disused limestone quarry of Greenleighton to the banks of Fontburn reservoir; treading the varied and scenic acres of Wallington Estate, by waymarked tracks and moorland paths. An historic experience ranging from a Bronze Age burial site and 'cup & ring' marks, Iron Age enclosures, Reiver incusions and the practices of nineteenth century agriculture climaxes with the viewpoint on Greenleighton Hill.*

Note: *This walk is only open to the walking public from 1 June to 30 October in order to protect the seasonal cycles of lambing and calving.*

Maps: OS 1:50 000 Landranger 81, Alnwick, Morpeth & surrounding area

National Trust Wallington Estates, Greenleighton Moor Walk brochure

Start/Finish: Greenleighton Quarry car park, GR 403591, 6½ miles (10.4km) NE of Wallington via a minor road NW from the B6342 just N of Rothley Lakes; signposted 'Greenleighton / Dyke Head'.

Distance: 6 miles (9.6km)

Height Gain: 340ft (104m)

Grade: 2½

Walking Time: 3½ hours

Accommodation & Parking:

A wide range of accommodation at Rothbury, 9 miles (14.4km) N via the B6342. Park at Greenleighton Quarry car park, GR 403591.

The Route: From Greenleighton Quarry (1) car park veer right, taking two right forks i.e. north keeping to the old track immediately alongside the quarried outcrops prior to swinging west via a ladder stile towards a shelter belt. At the tree line walk north alongside the trees for approximately 250yds/m, then turn left through the trees for a westerly stile-assisted passage through and beside various coniferous strips and plantations to the north of Greenleighton Farm.

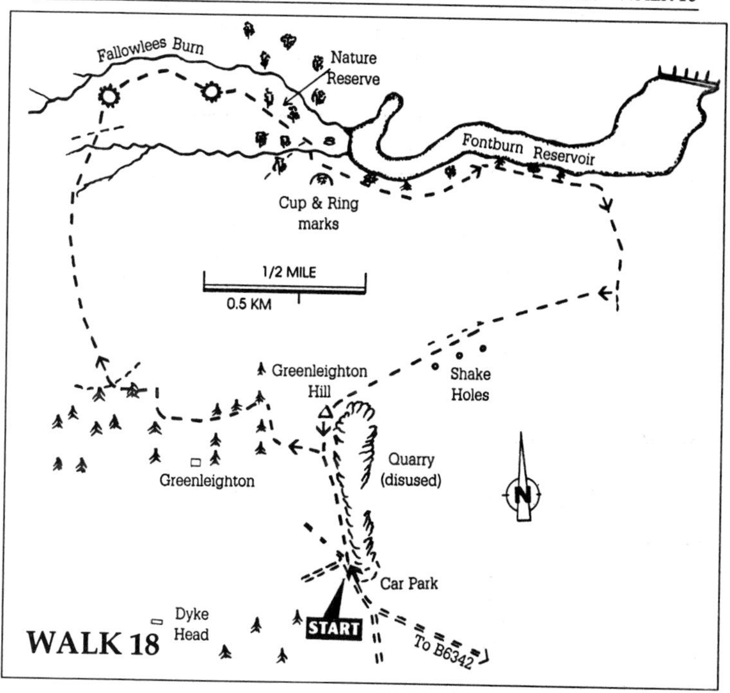

Once clear of the plantation, by stile, take the waymarked track north-north-west (not the bisecting bridleway) over the airy, scenic rough pasture and open moorland (2), descending gradually to a series of Iron Age enclosures above Fallowlees Burn. At the first mounded and ditched enclosure the way swings right fluctuating between east-north-east and east-south-east for 1¾ miles (2.8km) with the course of Fallowlees Burn, then by ladder stile through the broadleaves of Fallowlees Nature Reserve (3) to the southern treelined shores of Fontburn Reservoir. A delightful section, with a scatter of round sheep stells, that passes between an earthfast boulder inscribed with 'cup & ring' marks and a Bronze Age burial mound (4) prior to a wooded walk alongside Fontburn Reservoir (5).

Once clear of the wooded shore the route turns right onto open moorland, steadily ascending south for some 600yds/m before swinging right, i.e. south-west, initially with a public footpath, along a line of limestone Shake Holes (some fenced), leading to Greenleighton Hill trig point (6), 935ft (284m), above its scarred and quarried south-eastern flanks. A place to pause and savour the past as it overlooks Northumberland's wild moors and stark crags.

A few steps south from the viewpoint and we join, by ladder stile, our outward path for journey's end at the quarry car park.

ITEMS OF INTEREST ALONG THE WAY

(1) GREENLEIGHTON QUARRY. Limestone was quarried from this hillside from the early part of the eighteenth century, yielding some 2 million tonnes for agricultural lime production and road-stone prior to its closure in 1982.

(2) MOORLAND. A 'farmed' area of rough grazing, managed by the controlled ebb and flow of sheep and cattle over its upland acres, this traditional method being known locally as 'raking'. Today the pastures are encouraged with applications of lime and inorganic fertilisers.

(3) FALLOWLEES NATURE RESERVE. A quiet valley area covering 3 acres, rich in lime-loving flora such as broadleaved cotton grass, grass of parnassus and purple orchids, in addition to abundant birdlife, including the seasonal cuckoo. It is also home to the otter.

(4) BRONZE AGE REMAINS. 'Cup & Ring' marks are evident throughout the uplands of Northumberland, and can be found inscribed on earthfast boulders at Roughting Linn, Doddington Moor, Weetwood Moor and Lordenshaws. They consist of a cup-like depression surrounded by several inscribed concentric circles which are thought to relate to birth and death as they are often found in the vicinity of burial mounds. One theory as to their meaning suggests they are in fact 'plans' of Bronze Age forts/settlements, whose surrounding ditches and embankments bear an uncanny likeness to the concentric 'rings'. Burial mounds contained a stone burial box, or cist, which would be protected against scavenging animals by heaps of stones.

(5) FONTBURN RESERVOIR. Now run by Northumbrian Water it was originally built in 1910 to supply water to Morpeth, Ashington and Whitley Bay, at the rate of 5½ million gallons per day.

(6) GREENLEIGHTON HILL. The name Greenleighton is said to have originated from 'lytedun' - a beacon set on a hill. In medieval times such a beacon was in place to warn of the approach of Border reivers, coupled with a pele tower that stood close to the present day farm.

Walk 19: Wannie Line Walk
SCOTS GAP, ROTHBURY LINE & THE WANNIE LINE

Type of Walk: *A gentle circular journey that probes, by rail-bed and permissive paths, into the history and scenic highlights of the Wansbeck valley. Waymarked by white arrows the outward route is by courtesy of the Rothbury Line while the return travels with the sweeps of the Wannie Line. Between the two, our stiled and gated way crosses many burns through this tidy and orderly pastoral heart of Central Northumberland.*

***Note:** This walk is only open to the walking public from 1 June to 30 October in order to protect the seasonal cycles of lambing and calving.*

Maps: OS 1:50 000 Landranger 81, Alnwick, Morpeth & surrounds

Start/Finish: The National Trust Regional Office rear car park, GR 038864, 11¼ miles (18km) W from Morpeth via the B6343.

Distance: 7 miles (11.2km)

Height Gain: 279ft (85m)

Grade: 2

Walking Time: 3-3½ hours

Accommodation & Parking:
A full range at Morpeth, limited accommodation at Belsay. Car parking in the National Trust Office overflow car park, GR 038864.

The Wansbeck sings with all her springs.
The bents and braes give ear;

A.C. Swinburne

The Route: Walk north from the car park at the rear of the National Trust Office, swinging left, i.e. north-west onto the old rail-bed of

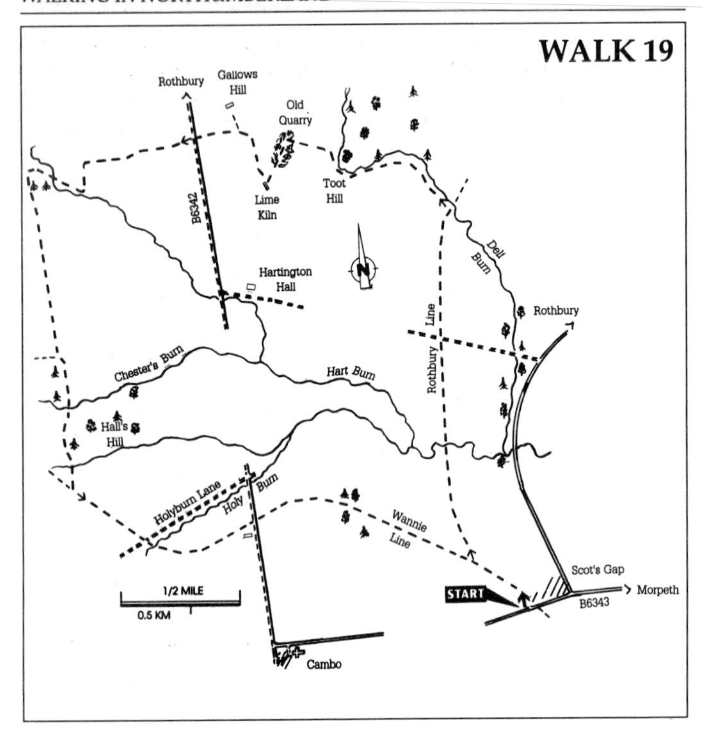

the Wansbeck Valley Line. The way soon arrives at Scot's Gap junction where the Rothbury Line (1) splits north from the westward sweeps of the Wansbeck Line (5), known to all as the 'Wannie Line'. Take the right fork as we walk due north through floral cuttings and on embankments for 1¼ miles (2km) to leave the rail-bed (2) as it swings right over Delf Burn.

At this tragic spot veer left to leave the Rothbury Line, and join the Delf Burn on a picturesque burnside path as it winds north and west. Leave the burn as it turns north below the tree clad Dorkin Rigg, crossing alongside stately beech, the Medieval Field markings (3) on Toot Hill to the stile leading to an old limestone quarry, complete with kilns (4), at its southern end. From the quarry and kilns make a U-turn north onto the old lime way, by the 250 year old beeches of Tuthill, originally linking north-west and west with Sir Walter Blackett's toll road, now the county road to Wallington.

Cross the road west for a waymarked fieldside walk. At the north-west corner of the third field, with more medieval field strips visible, turn right to walk south and join a track running north-west alongside Hart Burn. Cross the burn before swinging left, i.e. south for 1 1/4 miles (2km). Continue over Chester's Burn, by the walls and 'sod casts' and mixed woods on Hall's Hill, to join the rail-bed of the Wannie Line (5).

For 1 3/4 miles (2.8km) this well known line sweeps basically east to Scot's Gap, passing Holyburn Lane and Holy Burn to Rugley Walls alongside the road to Cambo (6). From this point the dominant tower of Cambo's Holy Trinity church can be seen, as one final sweep swings us into the closing stages, to the junction and journey's end at Scot's Gap.

ITEMS OF INTEREST ALONG THE WAY

(1) THE ROTHBURY LINE. 13 miles (20.8km) long, it reached Rothbury in 1870 having taken seven long years to construct. A single track branchline it carried coal, stone, lime and livestock as well as passengers before it closed after the second world war - in 1952 for passengers and finally freight in 1963.

(2) At this point a fatal accident occured in 1875, four quarrymen losing their lives when fully laden limestone trucks left the line and tumbled down the embankment.

(3) MEDIEVAL FIELDS. Distinguished by field strips of 'ridges and furrows'/'run and rigg', ploughed by teams of oxen working in a clockwise direction. A simple system of field drainage for the growing of cereal crops, that was practised in the county well into the eighteenth century.

(4) LIMESTONE & LIMEKILNS. These particular multi-pot kilns were built in the 1860s to replace previous single-pot kilns and were used to produce agricultural and industrial lime until the turn of the twentieth century. Limestone and coal, in alternative layers, would be fed into the 'pot' at the top of the kiln, a fire would then be lit in the grate below, the updraught igniting the coal above, and within a few days the first lime - 'quick lime' - would be ready. Such a sequence could be maintained for up to a year by topping the kiln

with fresh limestone and coal as the quick lime was drawn.

(5) THE WANNIE LINE. Originally the Wansbeck Valley Line, from Morpeth to Scot's Gap, which it reached in 1862 after six years of construction. It was later absorbed by the North British rail company and carried on to Redesmouth in 1865. It suffered closure, as did all of Northumberland's branchlines, with the last down-line run of the *Wansbeck Piper* on 2 October 1966.

(6) CAMBO. The village that educated Capability Brown, perhaps England's most distinguished landscape gardener, who in later life laid out some of the gardens and parks that grace Wallington House.

Walk 20: Classic Crags and Silver Birch
BOLAM LAKE, SHAFTOE CRAGS and DEVIL'S CAUSEWAY

Type of Walk: *A pleasing pastoral and moorland crag walk, through which public paths, country lanes and tracks lead from the parkland of Bolam Lake to the classic scarps and grandstand of Shaftoe Crags. Never demanding, highly satisfying, the scenic route strolls by Salters Nick, Pipers Chair, The Devil's Causeway and fourteenth century Shortflatt pele. Bolam Lake Country Park, a popular honeypot, attracts swarms of weekend visitors but few venture beyond the park boundaries.*

Maps: OS 1:25 000 Pathfinder 523, Morpeth West
OS 1:50 000 Landranger Sheet 81, Alnwick & Morpeth

Start/Finish: Bolam Lake Country Park, GR 083821, 2$^{1}/_{2}$ miles (4km) N from Belsay on a minor road from the A696(T)

Distance: 6 miles (9.6km)

Height Gain: 427ft (130m)

Grade: 2

Walking Time: 3 hours

Accommodation & Parking:
A range of accommodation in Morpeth and Belsay. Three car parks within the Country Park - honesty boxes request a nominal charge.

Hi, canny man hoy a ha'penny oot,
Me farther's in jail, and we canna get him oot.
We'll have some fun. there is ne doot,
Hi canny man, hoy a ha'penny oot.

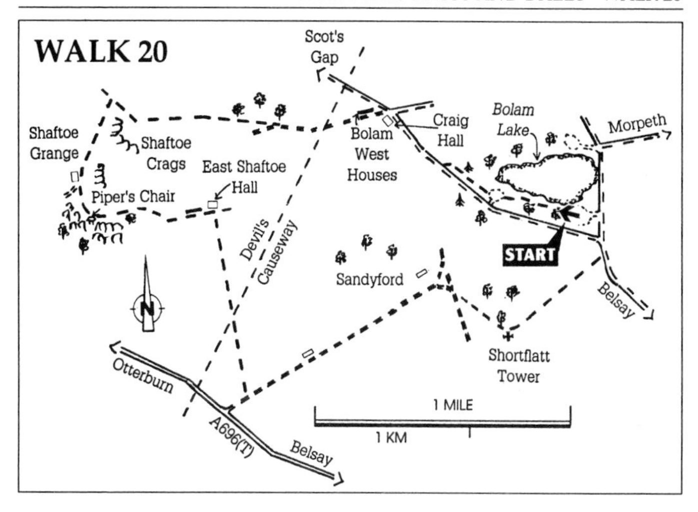

As this walk looks over the Wansbeck valley towards Morpeth this verse by Harry Nelson from a traditional Morpeth/Wansbeck children's song is appropriate.

The Route: Walk west from any of Bolam Lake's (1) car parks, via wooded lakeside prepared paths to join the Scot's Gap road beyond the western extremity of the lake. Turn right onto the tarmac for 1/2 mile (0.8km) of road walking, north-west, to the crossroads of Craig Hall and Bolam West Houses.

Turning left onto a coarse, stony, beech flanked track leading west beyond the row of cottages (note in the beech hedge their old communal water points) in the direction of the grassy flanks of Shaftoe Crags. After 1/2 mile (0.8km) veer right by the stone enclosed sheep dip, with a cairned tumulus, the flat top of Humilie Dod and the indiscernible course of the Devil's Causeway on the left, continuing to a cattle grid with white wicket gate. Pass through leaving the farm lane for a marginal pastoral path alongside a fine stone wall, enclosing rhododendrons and silver birch, rising west to rock strewn open pastures. As height is gained and Northumberland's endless acres are exposed, with Holy Trinity church, Cambo, particularly prominent, pass through a field gate leading into the crags and crevice of Salters Nick.

From this stony mini canyon walk west to a wall junction then turn left, i.e. south with the pathway flanked by guiding wall on the right and an explosion of sandstone crags left, to the farm of Shaftoe Grange. Here we fork left ascending south-east with the triangulation pillar (2) north of the track, and the mushroomed outcrop known as Piper's Chair (2) south of the track. Both provide bird's-eye views in all directions. Carry on east with the track, silver birch gracing our right flank, descending on the winding stone-paved 'destitution' road to pass through a gated wall to the walled garden and steading of attractive East Shaftoe Hall.

At the Hall swing right, i.e. due south for a pastoral journey of 3/4 mile (1.2km) by public path crossing stiles, a footbridge and the course of the Devil's Causeway (3) a few yards north of How Burn. South of the burn turn left, following the lane north-east beyond the tidy property of West Tofthill to the drive-end of the soft sandstone colours of Sandyford, typically Northumbrian. Ahead at the lane junction swing right and at the immediate finger post, 'Bridleway, Belsay 2 1/2 miles', leave the lane walking south-east, through silver birch surrounded pasture, toward Shortflatt Tower (4). Once over a footbridge and stile leave the bridleway left on a public footpath approaching Shortflatt, skirting the out-buildings by marked stile, wicket gate and footbridge.

With the medieval pele now behind, the fenceside footpath runs north-east for 3/4 mile (1.2km) by ladder stile, footbridge, step stile and paddock to the flower bedecked drive of Bolam Low House Farm opening onto the Belsay road. The final yards left take us over the road junction into Bolam Lake Country Park and journey's end; well perhaps not, for the encirling lakeside paths provide a pleasing finale.

ITEMS OF INTEREST ALONG THE WAY

(1) BOLAM LAKE & LAKE PLANTATION. The nineteenth century creation of J. Dobson, a Tyneside architect, who fashioned this pleasing place we see today from what was called in the local vernacular the 'splashy lands of Bolam'. The surrounding conifers and broadleaves are home to a host of wildlife including the red squirrel (emblem of the Country Park), badger, fox and shy roe

A Shaftoe Crags' spectacular

deer.

(2) PIPER'S CHAIR and its smaller immediate neighbours. Outcrops of weathered, banded Jurassic sandstone, shaped through time in the image of emerging mushrooms as a result of the softer bands being eroded more rapidly. Such geological contortions can be seen in the Bridestones on Bridestones Moor in the North York Moors. Among these crags dwell what are thought to be feral goats; they are in fact a little known breed of sheep - note the fleece is wool, not hair.

(3) DEVIL'S CAUSEWAY. A Roman Road spearing north through Northumberland from 'Corstopitum' by Corbridge to cross the Tweed at West Ord by Berwick-upon-Tweed. From above the footbridge over How Burn, the course of the road is just distinguishable on a bearing of 28° magnetic.

(4) SHORTFLATT TOWER. Not open to the public. Today's structure contains within the tower some of the original fourteenth century pele.

Walk 21: The Roman Memorial

HALTWHISTLE BURN, HADRIAN'S WALL, WALLTOWN

Type of Walk: *A varied walk through wooded dene and upland pastures to the whin sill scarps and crags that bear the great wall of Hadrian. Underfoot, waymarked burnside permissive paths, country lanes and tracks, public footpaths and bridleways journey by the industrial past of Haltwhistle and onto the 1900 year old phenomena of Roman military engineering. A journey packed with interest with a colourful abundance of wildlife, far seeing views, sightings of geological antiquity and relative solitude (as this route intentionally avoids the much visited honeypots).*

Maps: OS 1:25 000 Historical Map, Hadrian's Wall
OS 1:25 000 Pathfinder 546, Haltwhistle and Gilsland
OS 1:50 000 Landranger Sheet 86, Haltwhistle, Bewcastle & Alston

Start/Finish: Haltwhistle, GR 712643, adjacent to the A69(T) and the River South Tyne. Walk commences at GR 712643 from the signposted supermarket free car park.

Distance: 10 miles (16km)

Height Gain: 787ft (240m)

Grade: 3

Walking Time: 4½-5 hours

Accommodation & Parking:

A range of accommodation in and around Haltwhistle. Free car parking in Haltwhistle at GR 712643 by the supermarket. Free park and picnic site at Walltown, GR 668659, should you wish to reverse the walk.

For Hadrian's pride shall open lie
To bittern's boom and curlew's cry;
From Solway sands to mouth of Tyne
Vale is whispered on the Wall.

Howard Pease

The Route: From the supermarket car park turn right walking east on Willia Road to the houses of Fairfield Park. Immediately past the notice turn left, 'Public Footpath Pike Dyke Neuk 1/2 mile', passing by a wicket gate and descend right to cross a footbridge onto the east bank of Haltwhistle Burn. Rise to the cart track, turning left, and with the peat stained waters of the winding tree-lined burn journey in a northerly direction to pass the rather derelict pipeworks (1).

With the clayworks and signs of dark coals and shales behind, the dene narrows into gorge as the way passes by the foundations of a long-gone woollen mill. Continue with the flower strewn burn, all foam and froth in places and home to dippers and colourful wagtails, noting the angled exposures of sedimentary limestones and sandstones, beneath and behind the surrounding beech, birch and hazels. Haltwhistle Burn is crossed and re-crossed several times by footbridge; if in doubt at junctions and forks remain at all times alongside the burn to meet, beyond footbridge and wicket gate, mining memorabilia (2). Carry on along the old rail-bed, with crumbling limekilns (2) on either side of the burn, to cross the last footbridge, then by metal gate rise diagonally over a small pasture onto the B6318, the Military Road (3).

Turn right onto the verges of the busy Military Road for a brisk walk of 300 yards to the crossroads at Milecastle Inn. Turn left, signposted 'Cawfields', and follow the lane for 3/4 mile, turning left onto Haltwhistle Burn bridge and once over left by stone wall steps, signed 'Pennine Way, Chesters and Greenhead'. Ascend gradually north-west alongside stone walls, following Hadrian's Wall (4), to Great Chesters Farm. Little can be seen of the wall save the grassed

WALK 21

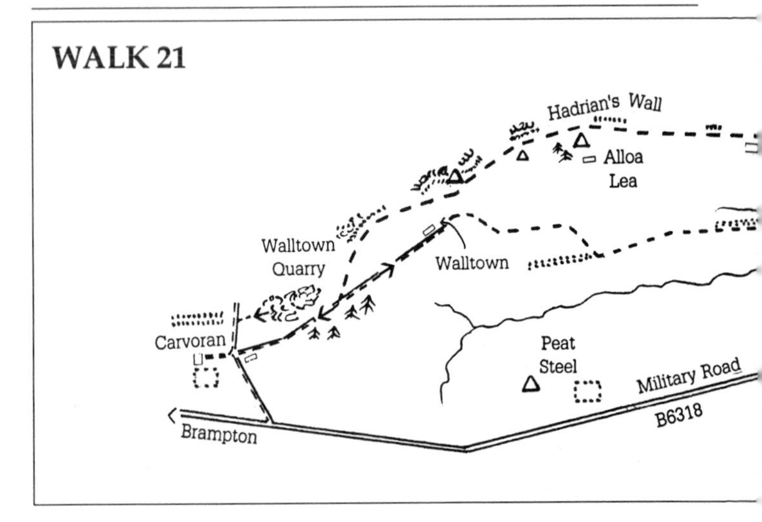

over foundations and northern ditches but it is of interest to note the large and symmetrical stones of an adjoining pasture wall! Great Chesters Farm marks the site of Aesica Roman Fort (5), a place of interest, before continuing west with the wall on a craggy switchback, so typical on this section of Hadrian's Wall. To the east the rearing outcrops of Winshields Crag, Steel Rigg and Sewingshields Crags divide the great Northumbrian wilderness, that nineteen centuries ago would have appeared to invading Scots as impenetrable, from the softer South Tyne valley to the south.

The approach to naked whin sill of Walltown Crags is, in addition to being an up and down affair, also a 'hands-on and feet-on' experience, as the path treads the foundations of the wall and passes Turret 44B (perhaps the best preserved turret of all). Descend left from Walltown Crags to join a woodside lane south-west (by the English Heritage information board) and then by cattle grid and gate onto a footpath to Walltown Quarry (6) and The Roman Military Museum at Carvoran.

Return, by path and lane, to the English Heritage information board and continue with the lane to Walltown Farm, centuries ago a fortified village. From here turn right with the tarmac strip

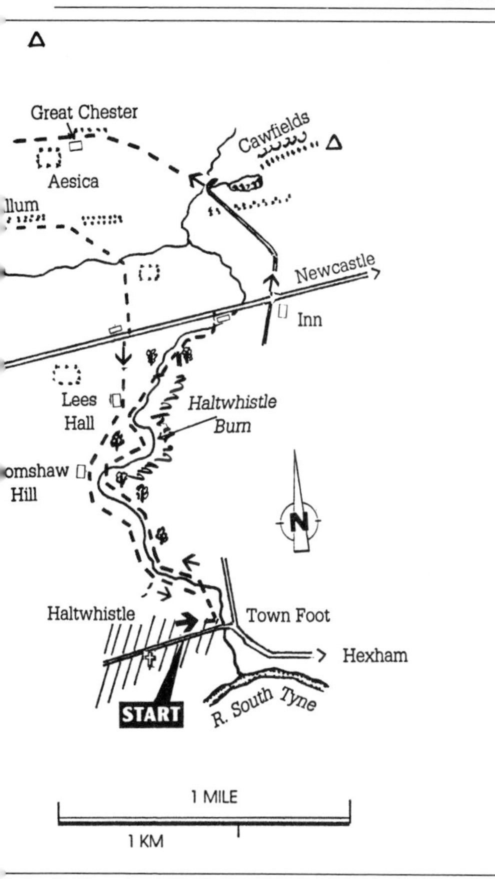

winding east, prior to running with the ditches and embankments of The Vallum (7) by cart track, below Alloa Lea Farm. The way reverts to tarmac south of Great Chesters Farm as it swings south to meet the Military Road.

Cross with care to the gated and signposted bridleway track descending south, past Lees Hall Farm with fine views into the gorge of Haltwhistle Burn, then by lane past Broomshaw Hill Farm, for a burnside return to Haltwhistle.

ITEMS OF INTEREST ALONG THE WAY

(1) TYNEDALE FIRECLAY WORKS. This one time contributor to the industrial wealth of Haltwhistle produced clay sanitation pipes, originally from locally quarried clay. In its latter days imported clay had to be brought in.

(2) With carboniferous seams close to the surface, coal was mined in this area from drift (tunnel) mines probing into the surrounding

hillsides and transported by wagon way to Haltwhistle. A restored chimney, wagon-way bed and ruined engine house bear witness. Ironstone and limestone were quarried nearby, no doubt also transported by the wagon way.

(3) MILITARY ROAD. Contrary to common belief this road does not relate to Hadrian's Wall or surrounding Roman roads. It is the much later product, circa 1752-3, of General Wade and his military road builders.

(4) HADRIAN'S WALL. Planned and built by Platorious Nepus, Governor of Britain on the orders of Emperor Hadrian, AD 122, as an unbroken barrier of stone and earth running 80 Roman miles (75 miles [120km]) from coast to coast. In addition to defensive ditches and embankments the Wall had attached forts and milecastles, with a turret between each milecastle. One interesting theory, discounted by the purists, as to reasons for the wall was not 'qui barbaros Romanosque divideret' - to separate the barbarians from the Romans - but to keep the barbarians from Rome's rich supplies of North Pennine lead ore.

(5) AESICA FORT. One of the Wall's smallest, it was built to protect the exposed Caw Gap. Excavated in 1894, outlines of a surrounding wall, store rooms and bathhouses (water supplied by aqueduct from Haltwhistle Burn) can be seen.

(6) WALLTOWN QUARRY. A major supply source of whinstone from 1871 to the 1970s it is now converted into a rich seam of geological information, a haven for indigenous wildlife, a nature trail and car park/picnic site with full facilities.

(7) THE VALLUM. A line of embankments and ditches running parallel to Hadrian's Wall, which marked the southern perimeter of the Wall's militarised zone.

Walk 22: River Allen by Gorge and Rigg
ALLEN BANKS, STAWARD RIGG AND CUPOLA BRIDGE

Type of Walk: *A linear passage through a National Trust beauty spot popular at weekends and public holidays. The waymarked way rises to the 'Bone Floor' then squeezes with the River Allen through the tree-clad narrows of Allen Gorge, prior to ascending Staward*

Rigg. Although tree cover filters sunlight and distant views, the sylvan mix is a joy, providing a symbiotic habitat for wildlife; note the birds, ferns and fungi. An all-seasons walk, a classic in spring and autumn.

Should a linear be inconvenient, return from Staward Peel via the banks of the Allen to Allen Banks.

Maps: OS 1:25 000 Pathfinder 546 & 547

OS 1:50 000 Landranger Sheet 87, Hexham, Haltwhistle (or Sheet 86)

Start: Allen Banks (National Trust), GR 797640, 3/4 mile (1.2km) S of the River South Tyne and the A69(T), and SE of Bardon Mill.

Finish: Cupola Bridge, GR 800592, carrying the A686 over the River Allen.

Distance: 5 miles (8km)

Height Gain: 534ft (163m)

Grade: 2

Walking Time: 3 hours

Accommodation & Parking:

Bardon Mill, Haltwhistle and Ninebanks youth hostel. Parking at Allen Banks.

Where can you find a fairer sight
By noon or eve or morning light
Than Catton's lofty height has shown
Or Staward, peerless beauty's throne

J. Ritson 1921

The Route: What better place to start this gorge and rigg walk than from the old walled garden of Ridley Hall, now Allen Banks car park with attached facilities; note the map and information board. Leave the car park and picnic area south with the waters of the Allen on our left, rising right at the first fork then right again to ascend south-south-west with the red waymarked path. Never too severe the track leads for 1/2 mile (0.8km) through the regal beeches above Raven's Crag, alongside the perimeter fence, to the cleared area of 'Bone Floor' sunhouse (1), between the red marker directing left and a fence corner.

Descend east, i.e. left through a wooded gully, favoured by red

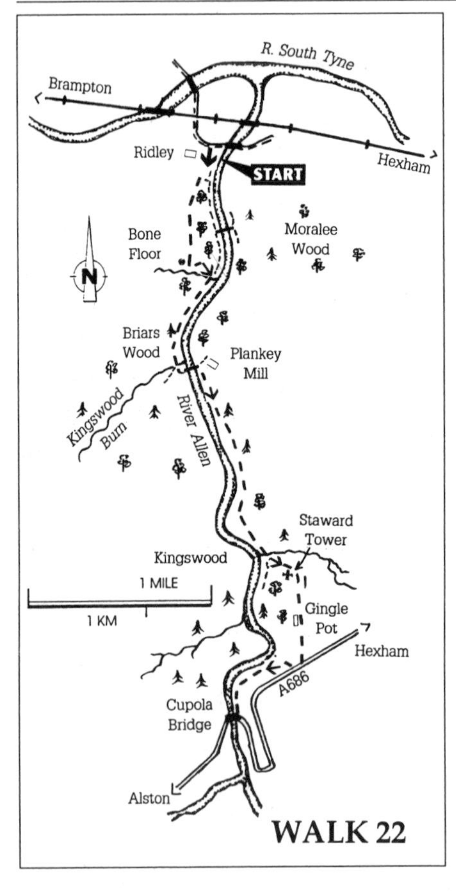

squirrel, via steep stepped zigzag onto the riverside walk alongside the rushing waters of a feeder burn. Turn right with the dark brown marker through an arboreal wonderland leading south-south-west to Briarwood Bank and Kingswood Nature Reserve (with informative wildlife panel); and finally to the oscillating suspension footbridge and the warm stones of Plankey Mill, a retired grain mill once powered by the waters of Allen.

Cross the Allen and turn right by stile and permissive path, through pastures, to a needle-strewn way right. The track, later shrinking to a pathway, follows the course of the river roughly south for 3/4 mile (1.2km) to cross Harsondale Burn, cascading west into the River Allen. At this point the river veers south-west away from the southbound gorge path and at the next fork swing sharp left onto a narrow, occasionally slippery, dirt pathway, rising, by a series of zigzags south-east, to meet the hefty stones in what is left of the north wall of Staward Peel (2) astride the eyrie of Staward Rigg. After a careful inspection leave the broken

Plankey Mill Farm

peel with the narrow ridgetop path south-east, and no matter how appealing the elusive views are stick to the path, for the drops of 250ft (76m) on either side to the Allen and Hartshorn Burn are immediate. Be patient as later heathery clearings allow fine sightings west into the Crooks of Allen and distant views north over the Tyne valley to the escarpments beyond Hadrian's Wall.

The wooded rigg is left, via a stile and flanking National Trust sign, for a wide pasture track, south-east and south beyond the remains of Gingle Pot to reach the A686 through a creaking fieldgate. Turn right for a quick 250yds/m scuttle alongside this busy road, escaping by ladder stile on the right to the relative safety of a pasture trod. Dropping north-west to the stile re-enter the wooded gorge. Once over take the left-hand descending public path, with yellow arrowhead, to the floor of Staward Gorge and the musical waters of the River Allen. Veer left, strolling alongside the true right bank of the Allen to journey's end by the three arches of Cupola Bridge (3), straddling the water-worn pavement of sedimentary rock below.

Flow on lovely Allen, through groves of rude grandeur,
Flow on, in thy serpentine course to the Tyne;
Anon.

ITEMS OF INTEREST ALONG THE WAY

(1) BONE FLOOR. This summer house, built by Susan Davidson of Ridley Hall in the mid 1800s, had as its floor hundreds of tightly packed leg bones of sheep. Arranged vertically in tight circles, with the knuckle bone uppermost, they provided a well drained dry floor, surrounded by stone flags, of 10ft (3m) diameter.

(2) STAWARD PEEL. Medieval in structure, although built of stone purloined from Roman ruins to the north. Not an easy task considering the age and the terrain to be traversed. Stout walls, a drawbridge and a portcullis gate were the orders of William Swinburne in 1278. The peel was later occupied by a local Tynedale reiver 'Dickie of Kingswood', of whom I know little. Below Staward Peel, by Cyphers Linn in a deep pool, lies legendary buried gold.

(3) CUPOLA BRIDGE circa 1778. A fine arched bridge, of local stone, named after a nearby lead smelting furnace. A 'cupola' was the name given to a furnace operating on the then revolutionary system of reverberation, a process of extracting metal from ore by means of evenly spread heat.

Walk 23: The South Tyne Line and 'Postman's Path'

LAMBLEY VIADUCT, RIVER SOUTH TYNE & FEATHERSTONE CASTLE

Type of Walk: *How pleasing are combined walkways of the Haltwhistle-Alston line railbed and the splendour of the Lambley Viaduct high above the winding banks of the River South Tyne to the parklands of Featherstone Castle. No windswept fells, weeping hags or industrial scars mar this circular waymarked pastoral stroll. A three-seasons photogenic walk on valley side and river bank in the company of an extensive and visible wildlife.*

Maps: OS 1:25 000 Pathfinder 559

OS 1:50 000 Landranger Sheet 86, Haltwhistle, Bewcastle & Alston

or OS 1:50 000 Landranger Sheet 87, Hexham and

Haltwhistle

Start/Finish: Featherstone Park South Tyne Trail car park, GR 682607. Signposted from the minor road junction at Rowfoot 550yds (0.8km) E.

Distance: 5 3/4 miles (9.2km)

Height Gain: 207ft (63m)

Grade: 2

Walking Time: 3 hours

Accommodation & Parking:
Haltwhistle and surrounds, also at The Wallace Arms, Rowfoot. South Tyne Trail car park (free), at Featherstone Park, GR 682607.

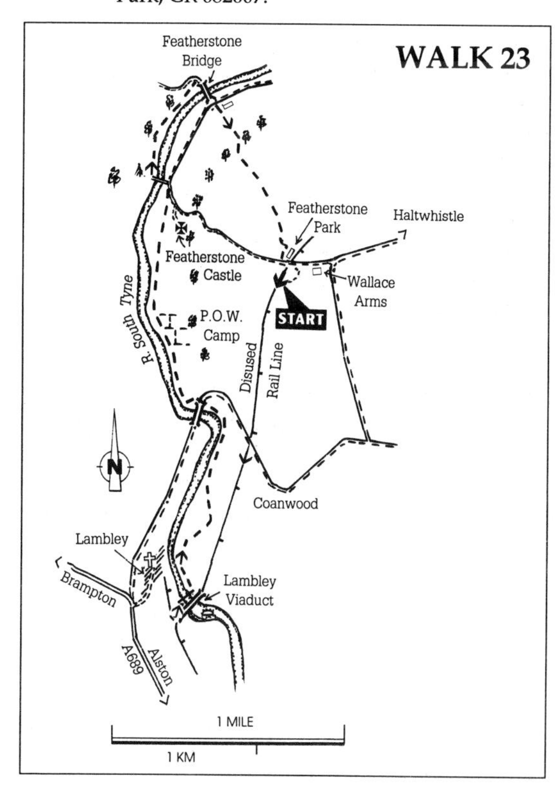

The Route: The car park by the old station of Featherstone Park (now a private house) provides a perfect start to this walk south-south-west, on the grass and ashes of the now defunct Haltwhisle to Alston branch line (1). Depart for a 1 3/4 mile (2.8km) gated waymarked journey to Lambley Viaduct, through undulating pastures flanked by stands of poplar, silver birch and mixed conifers; one of the few remaining habitats of the red squirrel. The species is sadly depleted elswhere by their aggressive grey cousins, but here fortunately kept at bay by the inhospitable surrounding fells.

By cutting and embankment the line strides south over the Coanwood-Lambley road, running between coppiced trees that provide bird's-eye views into the South Tyne valley, and opposite to the village of Lambley and its church of St Mary and St Patrick. Railway memories, such as buffers, stone stations, platforms and single sidings slide by, and now with gravel underfoot the step quickens as the roaring waters of the South Tyne are heard 140ft (43m) below and the recently renovated Lambley Viaduct (2) sweeps into view.

Access to the deck is through a single gate for a scenic crossing above the great rumbling sweep of the South Tyne below Hag Wood; vertigo sufferers are advised not to peer down over the parapets. Exit via a steep steel-stepped zigzag, at lower levels a wooden stepped pathway, to the west bank, swinging left to a new waymarked footbridge for a crossing to the east bank. Here admire the pillared, arched viaduct towering above the riverbed scatter of weathered and water-worn boulders.

Turn left with the footpath waymarks, keeping an eye open for emerging toads, to begin the 2 3/4 mile (4.4km) riverside stroll north beyond a 1940s POW camp and Featherstone Castle, to the single arch of Featherstone Bridge. A stretch that is perhaps the most pleasing of many in Northumberland, with musical waters and constant birdsong, graceful trees and carpets of wildflowers. Where even the piercing shrieks of alarmed oyster-catchers do not offend. Yellow arrowheads, 'public footpath', guide us to the tracked foundations and remaining brick buildings of POW Camp 18 (3) and onward by castellated Featherstone Castle (4) to a stone-stepped footbridge left, signed 'Bridge End 1/2 mile'. Over the now tranquil waters turn sharp right onto a woodland path leading to

Fontburn Reservoir (Walk 18)

Piper's Chair and Shaftoe Crags (Walk 20)

River Allen's Limestone Pavement at Cupola Bridge (Walk 22)
Featherstone Castle (Walk 23)

the elegant, single arch of Featherstone Bridge. Note the mason's mark on the parapet.

At the T-junction south of the bridge a waymark, 'Featherstone Rowfoot 1 mile' directs us south-east past the wall corner over haughs to the stepped ridge of coppiced trees ahead, a route known locally as the 'Postman's Path' (5). Once clear of the trees a series of stiled and waymarked pasture paths slope south-south-east to the corner of a coniferous plantation above the old station of Featherstone Park (6). The final stile steps into what was the station yard, but is now the private house garden. Turn half right, pass behind the house and exit the property by drive and roadside gate to the starting car park beyond. *The present owner of Featherstone Park is fully aware of the public footpath through his garden, and has no objections to considerate walkers who respect his property and keep to the public path.*

ITEMS OF INTEREST ALONG THE WAY

(1) HALTWHISTLE-ALSTON LINE. The line opened in 1852, a mere twenty-six years after the first stagecoach clattered into Alston, chugged along for 124 years and retired in 1976, despite much local protest. Goods carried were farm produce from the South Tyne Dale, coal from Lambley mines and lead from the levels surrounding Alston.

(2) LAMBLEY VIADUCT c.1852. The most spectacular relic of the age of steam on this walk, it is carried by 14 pillars (including the two massive bankside stanchions) and 16 arches (9 of which are in excess of 110ft [33.5m] above the South Tyne). During 1995-6 the viaduct was thankfully restored and is now in the hands of the North Pennines Trust.

(3) POW CAMP 18. A detention camp for thousands of German officers from 1945 to 1948. The interpreter from January 1946 was one Captain Herbert Sulzbach OBE who did much to cement relations between Britain and Germany.

(4) FEATHERSTONE CASTLE. Originally a defensive tower of the fourteenth century, home to the Featherstonehaugh family (who gave it its name) for many generations; it was extended to its present proportions in the 1800s by Thomas Wallace. The castle is not open to the public.

(5) POSTMAN'S PATH. This public footpath from Featherstone Bridge was originally the route used by postmen taking mail from the South Tyne valley around Featherstone Castle to the Haltwhistle train at Featherstone Park station.

(6) FEATHERSTONE PARK. In its day the main station between Haltwhistle and Lambley, and according to local memories, its siding provided an overnight stop for the royal train during the 1939-46 conflict, when duty called the royal family to Tyneside.

Walk 24: Flues and Chimney Stacks of the Silver Dale
ALLENDALE TOWN, RIVER EAST ALLEN & FLUE LINES

Type of Walk: *A circular walk from the old 'Frontier Town', by river bank and open fell, revealing not only the changing canvas of East Allen Dale and its indigenous wildlife, but also the ingenuity and insensitivity of the lead mining industry. A journey on public riverside paths, country lanes, moorland tracks and grassy trods, that is at times demanding but never exhausting. An historical and social experience, greatly enhanced when clear skies reveal the wild dales of East and West Allen.*

Maps: OS 1:50 000 Pathfinder 560, Allendale Town
OS 1:25 000 Landranger Sheet 86, Haltwhistle; or Sheet 87, Hexham

Start/Finish: Allendale Town, GR 837558, 7³/4 miles (12.4km) N of Allenheads by the B6295; 11¹/2 miles (18.4km) SW from Hexham via the B6303, B6304 and B6305.

Distance: 8³/4 miles (14km)

Height Gain: 1017ft (310m)

Grade: 3

Walking Time: 4¹/2-5 hours

Accommodation & Parking:
Allendale Town; parking spaces in the Market Place.

The Route: Unique Allendale Town (1) provides an ideal beginning, and end, for this varied walk. Descend west from the market place onto The Peth, signposted 'Thornley Gate & Ninebanks' and as the road curves left a footpath sign, 'Allenmill ³/4 mile' directs right, i.e. north. 300yds/m along the path we pass our first lead mining

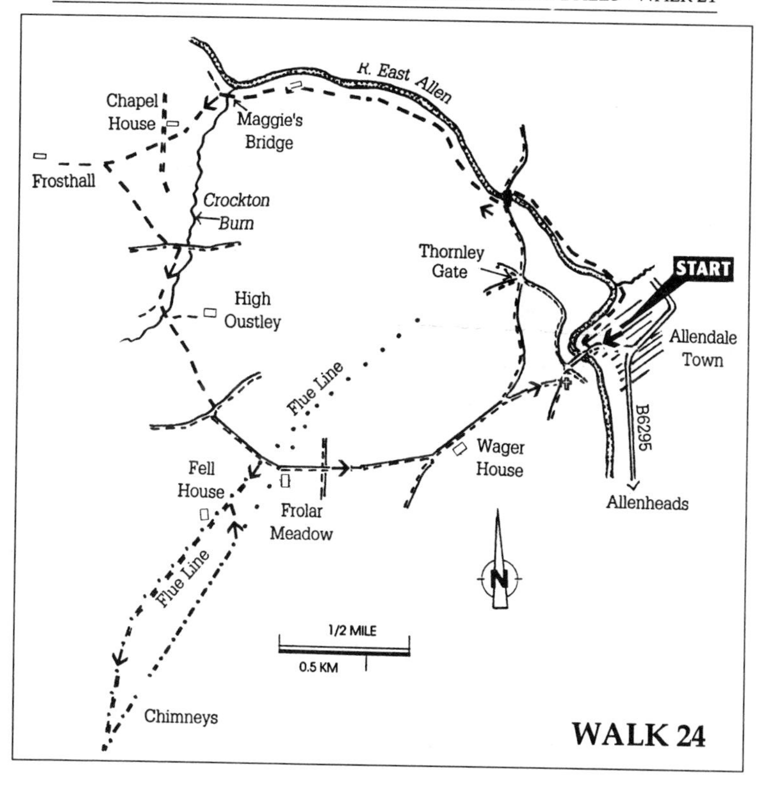

memorabilia, a ruined winding house and arched entrance to the 'Blackett Level' (2) prior to crossing Philip Burn. For the next mile our path follows the floral banks of the East Allen north-west for one mile to cross the roadbridge left, to Allenmill, site of the old smelt mills and starting point of the extensive Allenmill Flues (3), met later along the way.

As no visible evidence of the flues remains turn right onto the first tree-lined path, 'Oakpool 2 miles' through a wicket gate running north-west, always close to the river, for $1^{1/4}$ miles (2km). The way opens through stiled pastures, one with a clump of 5ft high tussocks, prior to rounding two uninhabited cottages and crossing Maggie's

Bridge over Crockton Burn, a wooden footbridge 'Opened by Margaret Shaw in 1983, from the Lads from Prudhoe CCTD'. The riverside path to the right is waymarked; our way (not initially waymarked) splits and ascends left, i.e. west-south-west to the dene rim via a distinct path. The path remains on the north side of the dene, now waymarked, to emerge onto a farm road south of Chapel House Farm.

Cross the road and by waymarked stile carry on west-south-west over walled pastures towards Hollybush plantation, turning left to walk roughly south with a wall through Rude Cleugh and pastures to reach the Thornley Gate / Ninebanks road by stile. Turn left walking east with the roadside verge for 200 paces then right over the marked stile 'High Oustley 1/2 mile'. Carry on south along the top tree line for 300yds / m then with a dirt path descend through coppiced trees to the dene floor, crossing Crockton Burn by footbridge. Once over take the marked right-hand path, rising steeply south-south-east between juniper and holly to the dene rim. Here a wallside trod plods through two pastures to emerge at a road T-junction. With quickened step, for the flues and chimneys are in sight, cross the road onto the lane, south-east for 550yds (0.8km) to the flues at Frolar Meadow junction. **Observe the Flue Lines with interest, but do not enter under any circumstances as they are unstable and unsafe.**

Turn right, i.e. south-south-west on a walled and gated lane to the open fell track, 'Public Bridleway, Chimney 3/4 mile', an old Carrier's Way (4), by Fell House. This ascending track runs with the flue line to the larger, more elevated but hidden chimney (5) ahead. A steady ascent provides close-ups of the arched and in places crumbling flue, plus panoramic views over East and West Allen Dales. Once reached and admired leave the partially restored chimney with an about turn north to the second chimney stack, higher in height, lower in elevation. Then by moorland pathway north-north-east alongside the more dilapidated flue, past a cemented stone cairn, gradually descend to swing left on a grass path leading to the outward lane below Fell House.

Turn right through the gate to the Y junction by Frolar Meadow Farm, taking the right fork east on a descending lane. At the crossroads carry on east by a wooded gully to pass Wager House,

Blackett Level

veering right onto a narrowing lane that descends and turns left to pass The Society of Friends Meeting House (6) prior to Mill Bridge over the River East Allen. Cross and ascend The Peth to the Market Place and its bevy of hostelries.

ITEMS OF INTEREST ALONG THE WAY

(1) ALLENDALE TOWN. Edward I granted the town's first charter, to what was to become the centre of East and West Allen Dale's prosperous lead and silver mining industry. In 1851 Allendale sent to the Crystal Palace Exhibition an ingot of silver weighing 345kgs. At this time the population rose to 6500 and all and sundry were attracted to this klondyke, in particular to 'The Pays', when miners received their biennial wages. Traditions live on to this day, with the colourful 'Old Year's Night' celebration of 'Tar Barling', a parade of (guisers) costumed people with burning tar barrels on their heads, releasing them only on the stroke of midnight to herald in the New Year.

(2) BLACKETT LEVEL. Planned by T. Sopwith, mine agent of the Blackett Beaumont Company. This crosscut tunnel, known as an 'adit', was constructed to assist exploration and drainage of the rich viens in Allenheads mines. Work started in 1855 and ceased in 1896, creating an 'adit' of 4$^{1}/_{2}$ miles (7.2km) and an outlay of £120,000!

(3) ALLEN MILL FLUES. Two arched flues stretching 2$^{1}/_{2}$ miles (4km) from the mills to the discharge chimneys, north of Black Hill. Built for commercial and humanitarian reasons in the late 1700s, 1) to create a controllable draught, essential to the Reverberatory Furnace system of lead smelting, and 2) to purify the air surrounding the smelters and prevent lead poisoning of people, stock and land. Sadly, little thought was given to the boys sent into the flues to clear the deposits of lead and sulphur.

(4) CARRIER'S WAY. A section of the packhorse route channelling in from the lead mines of West Allendale and Weardale Head to the Allen Smelt Mills.

(5) CHIMNEY STACKS. Imagine these two belching stacks on Allendale's skyline, the higher one, fed by two flues, with a ground level circumference of 30yds/m and the lower with its single flue some 10yds/m less. Such giants were required, as stated above, for both efficiency and health.

(6) FRIENDS' MEETING HOUSE. Originally built in 1733, this Quaker church or 'meeting house' was replaced in 1870. Graves of society members from far afield can be seen, as can the old lavatories, astride the beck.

Walk 25: Drovers, Miners & Monks
BLANCHLAND, BELDON BURN and CARRIER'S WAY

Type of Walk: *A waterside and fell experience, from one of the county's village gems, on and above Northumberland's southern perimeter, treading the ways of carriers, drovers, miners and monks. This lengthy circular journey, although by waymarked lanes, cart tracks and moorland trods of peat and stone, requires a modicum of mapreading skills and a feel for wild and lonely places.*

Maps: OS 1:25 000 Pathfinder 570, Allendale Town & Blanchland
OS 1:50 000 Landranger Sheet 87, Hexham & Haltwhistle

Start/Finish: Blanchland, GR 966504, on the upper Derwent, 12 miles (19.2km) S of Hexham via the B6306.

Distance: 11¼ miles (18km)

Height Gain: 820ft (250m)

Grade: 3

Walking Time: 5½-6 hours

Accommodation & Parking:
Hotel and B/Bs in Blanchland, varied accommodation in Hexham. A spacious car park 200yds NNW of the abbey.

The Route: From the village square of charming, timeless Blanchland (1), well worth a browse in its own right, walk south to the bridge, turning right by the last of the houses onto the riverside path leading west alongside the tree-lined true left bank of the river to the symmetrical arches of Baybridge. The Derwent and subsequent Beldon Burn provide the county boundary with Durham for the next 4½ miles (7.2km). At the bridge turn right onto the roadside and at the corner ahead veer left through the gateposts to Newbiggin Hall; yellow markers, 'public footpath, Riddlehamhope 3 miles'. Initially by lane the way passes a Wesleyan Chapel, circa 1869, prior to a continuum of walled pastures and pleasing views.

Newbiggin Hall is passed on the left as our way veers right, by

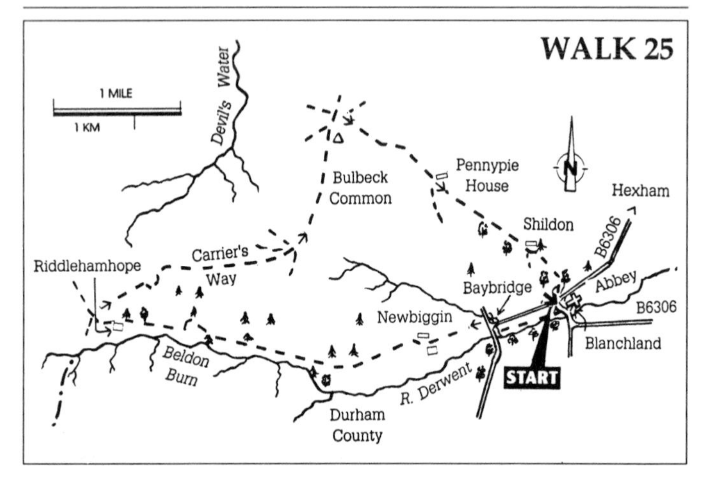

farm buildings, ascending to a marked gate and a well fed drinking trough. Carry on west along the gated track, past a shelter belt, and ignoring incoming paths continue above the isolation of Beldon Burn gully with the heather darkened slopes of Durham County's Nookton Back Fell to the south. The contouring route passes through the conifers of High Beldon and fringes those of Middle Plantation, just beyond which at GR 924498 is a trackside, half-hidden milestone (2) to Riddlehamhope. The now abandoned buildings of Riddlehamhope (3) are reached by a descending and ascending snaking way, north of Red Braes, that passes through a stiled finger of Scots pine.

Leave sad Riddlehamhope to the birds and vermin, walking west then north-west to embark upon the 'Carrier's Way' (4) at the marked style beyond the gate. Today a thin trod spears approximately north-east over the heather of Newbiggin Fell, to plunge into and through a glaciated steep-sided saucer, fortunately waymarked and with a wooden walkway. The bracken flanked north-east emergence rises and swings east onto a grass path through heather. A way that widens to a rutted, contouring track, over wild and exposed fells high above Devil's Water valley to the north, making for a solitary sportsman's hut ahead.

North of the hut and angled fence pass through the gate to two small cairns by a second gate for the stimulating rise, north-north-east over Birkside Fell, to the summit of Bulbeck Common, on good paths providing superb views. Here, some 400yds (370m) beyond the marked wall gate by cairned path, turn right i.e. south-east at the waymarked crosstracks over the quarried top of Bulbeck Common. Descending with moorland path and an excess of waymarks, pass over a wall by stile to the attractive long low buildings that are Pennypie House (5).

From this old drover's stop pass through a gate onto the farm road that descends south-east to the few houses of Shildon, with its mining remains, then by public footpath for a final and pleasing sylvan way into Blanchland.

ITEMS OF INTEREST ALONG THE WAY

(1) BLANCHLAND. Established by the Premonstatensian order, who from 1165 built the abbey and named it Blanchland, after the white habits of the monks. Today The Lord Crewe Arms occupies what were the abbot's house and kitchens. Booklets on the history of Blanchland are obtainable within the abbey.

(2) MILESTONE. One of many found alongside the old trade and drove stone-bedded routes. This one, inscribed 'RIM' arranged in an upright fashion, stands one mile from Riddlehamhope.

(3) RIDDLEHAMHOPE. A building that in its hayday obviously was more than a farmhouse, as can be seen by its design and size. The positioning and number of its windows are of interest, in particular the lack of them on north facing walls.

(4) CARRIER'S WAY. Ancient routes that ran from dale to dale, the country's commercial arteries, carrying by packhorse and occasionally horse drawn sleds the essentials and products of the area. In this southern sector of Northumberland vast quantities of lead ore (galena) were transported by packhorse (galloways) from mine to smelt mill.

(5) PENNYPIE HOUSE. Drovers, packhorse men and miners who, in centuries past, walked these wild and windswept moors would stop for sustenance and rest at moorland farmhouses along the way. This particular one gained fame with its pies that sold for a penny each.

Walk 26: Northumberland's Klondyke
WILD WEST ALLEN DALE

Type of Walk: *An up-hill down-dale fine weather circuit of the pitted and pimpled head of West Allen Dale, overlooked by the blackened bulwarks of Killhope Law, Northumberland's southern bastion. Here isolation reigns, with little company save that of the ubiquitous Swaledale, moorland birds, lead mine ghosts and a plethora of distant vistas. The route, by waymarked carrier's ways and thin heather trods, is both challenging and rewarding.*

Maps: OS 1:25 000 Outdoor Leisure Map 31, North Pennines
OS 1:50 000 Landranger Sheet 86, Haltwhistle, Alston
or OS 1:50 000 Landranger Sheet 87, Hexham, Haltwhistle

Start/Finish: Coalcleugh, GR 802453, 1½ miles (2.4km) S from Carrshield and 2 miles (3.2km) NE of Nenthead

Distance: 5½ miles (8.8km)

Height Gain: 919ft (280m)

Grade: 3

Walking Time: 3½-4 hours

Accommodation & Parking:
Allenheads, Nenthead, inns and B/Bs; plus Ninebanks youth hostel. Park at the road junction lay-by, GR 802453.

From the far off southern rim
Where the hills loom dark and grim
West All'n Water fair yet bleak
Downward flows a silver streak.

J. Ritson 1921

The Route: So remote is Coalcleugh and the crinkled outlook so dour, you may question your sanity as you walk west from the Allenheads/Carrshield junction. Go first via the mine track and mine shop of Coalcleugh Level (1) then by ford cross the infant River West Allen, above a small waterfall in Alston Cleugh. The track continues through grass covered spoil heaps, forking left with the marker to rise on a narrowing pathway with the waymarks to the boundary wall dividing Northumberland from Cumbria.

Ignore Cumbria's gated invitation by turning right, i.e. north with the wall for a hundred yards or so to the bridleway post, the

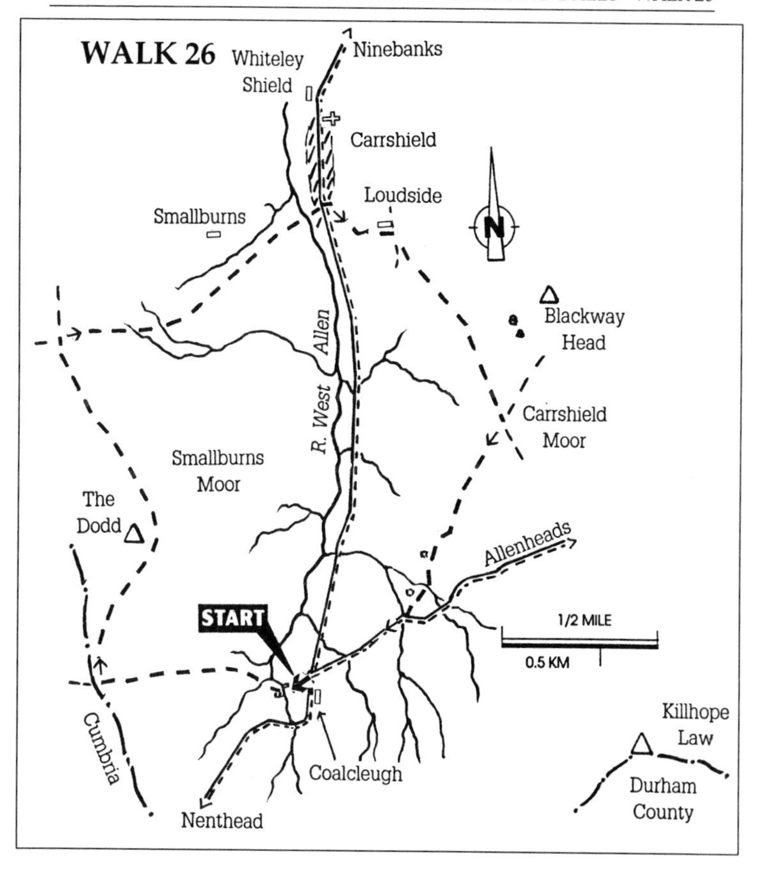

first of several guiding us north, on a tussock trod, to Dodd's End. Here a wider miner's track ascends The Dodd with ease, revealing the pleasing aspects of West Allen Dale, a lead and zinc mining dale whose past is reflected by the placenames met along the way. Coalcleugh Level, Peter's Pit, Carrier's Hill, Miner's Rest, Temperence Farm and Shivery Hill each have a tale to tell.

From The Dodd a grooved ridgeway track, a sure sign that the carrier's lead-laden galloways passed this way, surges north-north-west through tussock and sparse heather to a four-fingered 'Bridleway' signpost. Take the right finger, i.e. east over the descending tussock and heather rigg. The pathway, although ill-defined as it passes the wetlands by Gorcock Springs, is assisted to the stonewall corner by four strategically placed waymark posts. Stone dykes enclose the in-bye pastures of Smallburns Farm, seen on the left, and act as guides for the bridleway now dropping north-east to the abandoned Miners Rest. Beyond, the bridleway travels through an ill-drained rush infested enclosure to the footbridge over the lively River West Allen to rise between the cottages into Carrshield, an interesting lead mining village that is worth inspecting; note the village school (2).

Leave Carrshield at its southern end, by signpost 'Carrshield Moor 1 mile' and a cobbled way, south-east through two pastures to negotiate the deserted walls and pens of Loudside; turn right onto a farm track for a yard or so, before ascending left with a grooved way over and above quarry spoil and worked-out quarries. Although not too clear in places, the bracing bridleway to Carrshield Moor crosses the contours below Three Curricks (there are now only two) on Blackway Head. Ascend over open ground, on a bearing of 155° magnetic, to a lone marker post on the immediate horizon. Here the miner's track to Allendale's smelt mills, known by some as 'Black Way', is met.

Turn right onto this pathway towards the dark side of Killhope Law (3), capped by a single pine pole and currick; descending past the sad and abandoned ruins of Rushymea and Whetstonemea, to reach Bridge Cleugh and Allenheads road. The final yards west to Coalcleugh, by roadside verge and Mutton Hall, are greatly enhanced by the distant hazy vistas, 'fair yet bleak', of West Allen Dale's lead-bearing fells and geometric in-bye pastures.

ITEMS OF INTEREST ALONG THE WAY

(1) COALCLEUGH LEVEL / MINE. A large and rich mine, producing lead ore (galena) from the early eighteenth century to the present century. It replaced its pit-ponies with German engineered underground locomotives. The output of the mine and the extent of the underground 'levels' (tunnels) can be gauged from the all pervading spoil heaps that cover the dale head.

Large rubbish heaps along the hillside show,
The vast extent of hollow ground below.
Richard Watson

(2) CARRSHIELD. A company town, the company being the lead and silver producing Blackett Beaumont Company who held the main mining leases in Allendale and Weardale. A considerate employer, it built schools 'for the education of children of all religious denominations'; one such school, still standing, was built in Carrshield in 1851.

(3) KILLHOPE LAW 2209ft (673m). The highest on Northumberland's southern boundary this sombre mountain, capped by a triangulation pillar, an impressive pine pole and coned currick, has a foot in two counties and surveys a third. Regardless of its outline it bears a remarkable resemblance underfoot to its higher northern counterpart, as addictive bog-hoppers will confirm.

Walk 27: Highs and Lows of the Silver Dale
ALLENHEADS, RIVER EAST ALLEN TO HIGH HADDOCK STONES

Type of Walk: *From revitalised Allenheads, the route explores the dale's floor and its man-fashioned flanks for an insight into the life and times of the lead miner. Making use of Carrier's Ways and mine tracks, the public paths make light of daleside ascents. A quiet journey with riverside and moorland wildlife, which, now the clamour of smelt mill and mine has subsided, is flourishing.*

Maps: OS 1:25 000 Outdoor Leisure Map 31, North Pennines West Sheet

OS 1:50 000 Landranger Sheet 87, Hexham, Haltwhistle and surrounds

Start/Finish: Allenhead's Heritage Centre, GR 859453, 8 miles (12.8km) S of Allendale Town via the B6295.

Distance: 7 miles (11.2km)

Height Gain: 919ft (280m)

Grade: 3

Walking Time: 4 hours

Accommodation & Parking:

Available in Allenheads and Allendale Town, plus Ninebanks youth hostel. Car park opposite Allenheads Heritage Centre.

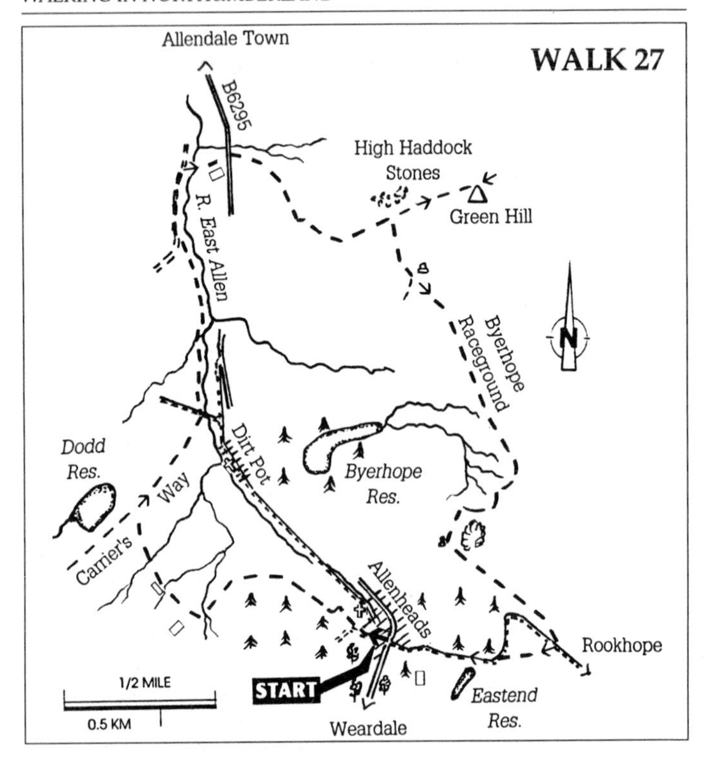

The Route: North-north-west from Allenheads Heritage Centre (1) rise with a cart track, left of Allenheads Inn (an Aladdin's cave), to a fork by The Blacksmith's Shop. Carry on straight ahead with the walled track towards a disused chapel, leaving the chapel lane through a waymarked gate for a path between forest fence and stone wall. At the gated cottage ahead turn sharp left on a narrow waymarked trod, crossing two stiles before turning sharp right onto a forest path north-west through School Plantation. The rounds and mounds of lead spoil, now visible below, indicate the intensity of mining activity centuries ago.

By stepped stile our waymarked path swops sides as we continue west-north-west then north by pastures to the lane rising over the 'hushed' ground to West End Farm. At the entrance leave the lane for a waymarked fenceside path north-west by the silent walls and sightless windows of Viewly Hall. Not a Hall in the recognized sense but a local dales name for a farmhouse, of which Viewly is typical; farmer/miner, family and animals all under the same roof, but, unlike the Longhouses of North Tynedale, with two separate doors. Once over Blackcleugh Burn the track ascends north to the Carrier's Way (2), just below Dodd Reservoir (3). Swing right onto this historic grassy Way, looking down to the roofs of Dirt Pot (4) and the River East Allen.

Do not cross the musical waters, but swing left with the tarmac for approximately 100yds/m, to a public footpath marker directing north over mine-scarred pasture. At the first fork veer right to the river bank onto a narrow path ambling between stone walls and River East Allen to a signposted country lane. The sign informs us we have come from 'Dirt Pot 3/4 mile'. Swinging right and dropping to the riverside, cross by footbridge or ford, to ascend alongside cottages and at 'Fell View' cross the B6295.

Pass through the waymarked wicket gate onto a winding, marked miner's track plodding south-east and east through the grassed-over spoil of yesterday's lead mines. After 3/4 mile (1.2km) and 460ft (140m) of ascent Byerhope Bank is reached, identified by a right-hand incoming path and a shoal of weathered outcrops, High Haddock Stones (5), on the left. If the day is clear and the spirit willing a far-seeing diversion can be enjoyed by continuing east onto 'Broad Way' for 550yds (500m) to the watershed of Green Hill, 1736ft (529m), for views east to Beldon Burn, Upper Derwent Dale and their surrounding moors (Walk 25). Return to the pathway junction with its triple marker-post by the Haddock Stones.

Descents and contours predominate as we drop south over quarry scarred Byerhope Bank to the prominent cairn at the junction above Byerhope Farm. Take the left fork for the wall corner by 'Byerhope Raceground' for a wall guided track over Byerhope Mere to Middle Rigg, allowing views west of the mined moors of Allen Dale to Killhope Law. Traverse Middle Rigg south-west, with its sad collection of abandoned farms (6), on a contouring track, crossing Noble Sike, to the large working quarry.ahead. It is best to go to the cairns/curricks right of the track and enjoy the views over

Allenheads and the moorlands leading to Durham and Cumbria.

With the heavy-duty quarry track hurry south-east to meet the Allenheads-Rookhope road. Cross and with the waymarks descend west by Eastend Burn, a roadside cairn and Eastend Reservoir, walking with the tree-lined road into Allenheads, and on to Allenheads Inn.

ITEMS OF INTEREST ALONG THE WAY

(1) ALLENHEADS. Lead and silver mining and smelt mills created this, the highest village in England; indeed in the year 1869 the twin dales of Allendale extracted 1$^{1}/_{2}$ metric tonnes of silver from the lead ore. Read all about it at today's Heritage Centre, which details the industry from the late 1700s. Exhibited also is the sole survivor of nine hydraulic engines designed and built by W.G. Armstrong in 1852 for use in Allen Dale's mines. The same W.G. Armstrong was connected with Rothbury's Cragside and Bamburgh's Castle.

(2) CARRIER'S WAY. Strings of packhorses, known locally as 'galloways', each carried 16st (102kgs) of lead ore to the belching smelt mills surrounding Allenheads. The resultant 'pig-iron' from the smelt mills was also carried by the sturdy galloways to a rail head or foundry, a practice that continued into the 1880s.

(3) DODD RESERVOIR. One of many surrounding Allenheads - Eastend, Byerhope and Coatenhill can still be seen. Built to feed the need for power as lead production increased, they supplied the great water wheels and machinery that served Allenhead's mills and mines.

(4) DIRT POT. A company-built miner's village, with two Methodist Chapels, one a Wesleyan Methodist, the other a 'Ranter's' Chapel - Primitive Methodist. Social historians will no doubt recognise the absence of a C of E church.

(5) HIGH HADDOCK STONES. I can find no explanation for this fishy name, save that the scatter of sandstone may have been thought to resemble a shoal of haddock. Or could it have been that 'haddock' is a local distortion of 'paddock'.

(6) FARMING MINERS. Or Mining Farmers. The abandoned steadings, such as those on Middle Rigg and West End Allotments, were small farms worked by the entire family; known in the dales

as 'Three acres and a pig' or as 'Pigs, potatoes and poultry'. The mining of lead however took priority, with the farm only fully staffed at hay time. Indeed it was expected that the children would work at the 'Washing'.

> *The ore's awaitin' in the tubs, the snows upon the fell,*
> *Canny folks are sleepin' yet but lead is reet to sell.*
> *Come on my little washer lad, come let's away,*
> *We're bound down to slavery for fourpence a day.*
>
> *The Washer Boys.* A mining song

CHAPTER 3
Northumbrian Shores

And now the vessel skirts the strand
Of mountainous Northumberland;
Towns, towers and halls, successive rise,
And catch the nuns delighted eyes.
Sir Walter Scott, *Marmion*

Running south from the sands of Cocklawburn Beach to Tynemouth's ruined priory is the lustrous jewel in the county's crown, immortilised by A.C. Swinburne in *A Jacobite's Exile* as the 'Lordly Strand of Northumberland.' Endless empty miles of sandy bays, rippling dunes and rocky points that bear the pages of Northumberland's history. For here was the cradle of northern Christianity, the death-bed of saint and sinner and site of silhouetted coastal castles where Northumbrian kings were crowned. Today its cliffs, rocks and adjacent Farne Islands are home to innumerable colonies of sea birds and seasonal migrants.

From the Tweed estuary south to Amble, where the Coquet meets the sea, nestle a series of fishing villages. Most are small with dwindling numbers of active fishing boats and only Craster can claim a natural harbour. They all have however one great natural resource, the hardy breed of Northumbrian fishing communities.

So extraordinarily unique is this bird-watcher's paradise that it was in 1958 declared an Area of Outstanding Natural Beauty while the area surrounding and including Holy Island (most of) and Budle Bay is a National Nature Reserve. South from Amble the shoreline bears the scars of industrial Tyneside's past, and its present, from Newbiggin-by-the-Sea, Blyth and Seaton Sluice to the 'Kiss-me-Quick' holiday resorts of Whitley Bay and Cullercoats.

THE WALKS

The walks, for all seasons, are contained within a coastline of 48 miles (76.8km), although they traverse a total 59 miles (94.4km) due to forays inland and riverbank walking.

Half of the eight walks included in this chapter are linear and may, if return transport is arranged / available, be treated as such. One walk, from Budle Bay to Seahouses, can, by retracing one's steps, be turned into a 'there-and-back' walk. But most exciting of all, the walks can be linked together for a fascinating continuous coastal trek into the sun, from Berwick-upon-Tweed to Warkworth. Care is needed however when timing walks along the beach sections to avoid high water, as public paths / bridleways do not run with the coastline for its entire length.

Walk 28 sets the ball rolling with a historical and scenic circuit of Berwick's Elizabethan Walls, with **Walk 29** encompassing the silvery Tweed estuary and its three fine bridges. **Walk 30** provides the easiest 13½ miles (21.6km) in Northumberland as it seeks out the 'Lordly Strand' and the Pigrim's Way to Lindisfarne with **Walk 31**, a short but sweet scenic circuit from village, harbour and castle to Emmanual Head. Starting at the Nature Reserve of Budle Bay, **Walk 32** passes beneath the awesome shadow of Bamburgh Castle and within sight of the scattered Farne Islands, bound for Seahouses. **Walk 33** is again one of those glorious 'short-long' beach walks, this one from the tiny harbour of Beadnell via the golden sands of Beadnell and Embleton Bays to Castle Point and the silhouetted stones of Dunstanburgh. The Craster Round, **Walk 34**, leaves Craster, an internationally renowned kipper village, for a coastal and pastoral circuit to the village of Longhoughton. Finally **Walk 35** provides a fitting finale with a circuit of Alnmouth, a splendid beach walk and a browse alongside the meandering Coquet, through Warkworth's byways to Hotspur's castle.

Walks 28: The Elizabethan Walls and 29: The Silver River
BERWICK-UPON-TWEED

Type of Walk: *Berwick marks the start of two walks. One encircles the town via its medieval and Elizabethan walls, fishing harbours and stepped quays; the second ramble, somewhat longer, leaves via the old Berwick Bridge to journey by the sweeping banks of the Tweed, the queen of rivers. For those who wish, the two can be combined to form a delightful town and riverside ramble.*

Berwick, a frontier town, was, prior to the late thirteenth century, a major Scottish seaport and much fought over, changing hands no less than fourteen times before finally falling to the English in 1482.

Maps: OS 1:25 000 Pathfinder 438, Berwick-upon-Tweed
OS 1:50 000 Landranger Sheet 75, Berwick-upon-Tweed

Start/Finish: Berwick-upon-Tweed old Berwick Bridge, GR 997528 - at Bridge Street/ Quay Walls junction. Berwick stands 3 miles (4.8km) S from the Scottish border line.

Distance: Town Walk 4 1/4 miles (6.8km), including the Pier; River Walk 4 3/4 miles (7.6km)

Height Gain: Minimal for both walks

Grade: 2

Walking Time: Town Walk 2 1/2 hours; River Walk 3 hours

Accommodation & Parking:
A range of accommodation in Berwick and adjoining Tweedmouth and Spittal, plus central car parks (pay)

At Tweidis mouth thair standis ane noble toun,
Into this toun, the quhilk is callit Berwik

Dunbar, *The Freiris of Berwick*

The Town Walk Route

As Bridge Street joins the old Berwick Bridge (1) veer left onto the worn flagstones of Quay Walls (2), overlooking the old quay and the Tweed's tidal estuary. Pass Sallyport and Shore Gate (3), the Customs & Excise House and an eighteenth century Guardroom. Once beyond Shore Gate, Quay Walls gives way to the Berwick Ramparts (4).

Left of the ramparts note the imposing Wellington Terrace whilst ahead the intriguing structures of Coxon's Tower and Fisher's

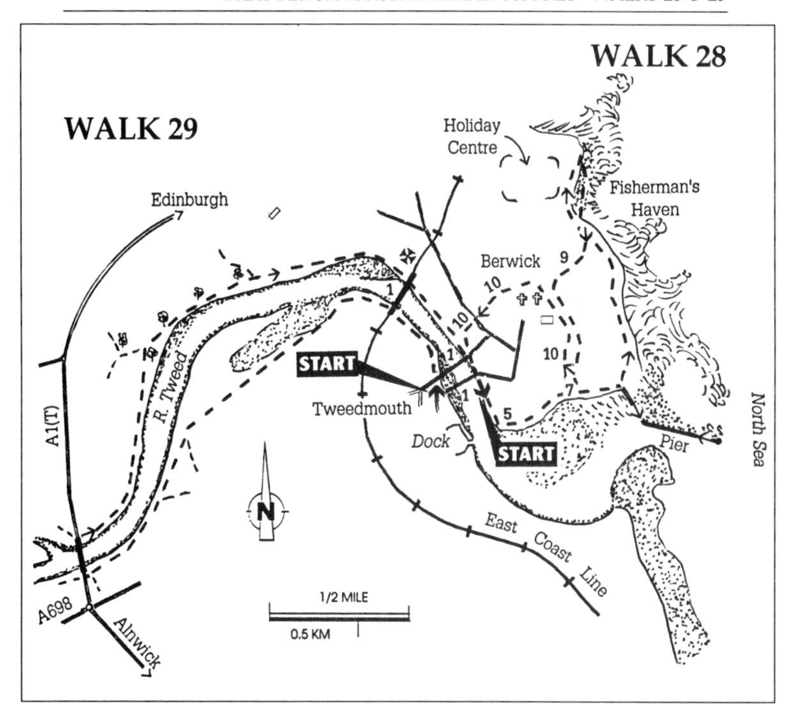

Fort (5) provide interest and inviting views south of the estuary, Spittal and the distant coastline to Lindisfarne and Bamburgh castles. Beyond Coxon's Tower the wall path veers north-east by Fisher's Fort to reach Berwick Pier/Ness Gate (6).

Leave the wall to pass through Ness Gate, east below the staunch walls of King's Mount (7) and between the terraced houses and the estuary rocks, to the landward end of the pier. On a fine day this $^1/_2$ mile angled breakwater provides a pleasing extension, offering seldom seen views of Berwick and its surrounding coastline.

Opposite a small car park the lane between Pier House and Meadowhaven Cottage rises to the southern extremity of Magdalene Fields golf course. Leave the tarmac and swing right onto a grassy fenceside public path north, above the shoreline strata of Bucket Rocks and Ladies Skeers, to a raised redoubt (now a golf tee) of the

Covered Way (9). Here a curving road leads to the corner of Berwick Holiday Centre, and to the right a dirt path skirts above Fishermen's Haven (8) to Sharper's Head. Return from this viewpoint descending left, via steep steps, to the small jetty and sandy cove before ascending a stepped way to the south. Swing left onto the tarmac path, then right, to cross the Covered Way (9) along its embankment (beware flying golf balls) to the road beyond the Bowling Club.

Turn left onto the winding road, and prior to Cow Port, left again following the path south over the Ditches (additional defences, now overgrown) on the seaward side of Windmill Bastion. As King's Mount is approached turn right through a stepped tunnel, circa 1895, to join the Elizabethan Walls (10) north and west.

Note Lion House, its entrance flanked by two stone lions of Venetian ancestry, and the buttressed walks and low pitched roof of the magazine - munitions store. Windmill Bastion (10) is met again, with the eighteenth century barracks visible within the walls, before Cow Port, circa 1750 appears. For centuries cows were taken daily, from within the town, through this gate to the pastures of Magdelene Fields - site of the Hospital of St Mary. The practice lasted until the 1940s. From Cow Port to Brass Bastion (10), observe the unique 1650s Cromwellian Holy Trinity Parish Church, with no spire, and Ravensdowne Barracks, headquarters and museum of the King's Own Scottish Borderers. Beyond, the bastions of Cumberland and Meg's Mount (10) follow in quick succession as Scots Gate, above the old A1 road, is crossed to Meg's Mount high above the Tweed. A splendid viewpoint from which to enjoy Berwick's river, three bridges, red pantiles, chimney pots and coastline.

From Meg's Mount descend south with Bankhill, by Lady Annie Gerningham's statue, to pass below the pillared supports of the Royal Tweed Bridge (1) before reaching the arched deck of Berwick Bridge (1), our initial starting point. A time to reflect on the verse, attributed to Robert Burns, regarding the 'noble toun callit Berwik'.

A bridge without a middle arch,
A church without a steeple,
A midden heap in every street
And damned conceited people.

Surely not.

ITEMS OF INTEREST ALONG THE WAY

(1) BERWICK BRIDGE. The oldest of Berwick's three bridges, with 15 stone arches of varying heights, begun in 1611 and completed in 1634. Its predecessors had collapsed due to the excesses of passing armies and the force of the sea. It was over this bridge that the Great North Road, from London to Edinburgh, ran until 1928; and where the bridge runs into Bridge Street there once stood English Gate - a monumental arch peacefully demolished in 1825.

(2) QUAY WALLS. A pleasing section flanked on the left by tight packed merchant's houses of the eighteenth to nineteenth century, overlooking the old quay.

(3) SALLYPORT & SHORE GATE. Sallyport is an original passage or 'port' leading through the wall from the quay to Bridge Street. Shore Gate, one of the main gates or 'ports' in the town walls was built in the mid-1700s and still retains its studded wooden doors.

(4) BERWICK RAMPARTS. Built on the site of medieval walls that ran south and west, along the waterfront. By each port in the wall nine, now grassed over, cannon mounts can be seen. They were installed around 1745 as protection against possible Jacobite incursions from the north.

(5) COXON'S TOWER & FISHER'S FORT. Coxon's Tower, a 'quarter-round tower' with four gun ports to the east and the Saluting Battery of thirteen ports to the west. Fisher's Fort, circa 1523, first known as 'Bulwark of the Sands', housed six cannon. Among the scattered ordnance stands a Russian cannon, captured in the Crimea.

(6) NESS GATE & BERWICK PIER. The gate was constructed under the Elizabethan ramparts in 1815/16 to facilitate the building of Berwick Pier. An impressive, elbowed breakwater, designed and built 1808-21 by John Rennie, whose elegant prototype for his Waterloo Bridge can be seen spanning the Tweed at Kelso, 25 miles west of Berwick.

(7) KING'S MOUNT. What views of the coastline this incomplete fort provides. It was named in honour of James VI of Scotland in 1603, as he journeyed south through Berwick to claim the English throne.

(8) FISHERMEN'S HAVEN. The old fishing harbour of Low Greenses (the fishing village of Berwick). A century ago thirty-six cobles

sailed from Fishermen's Haven; today one rides by the jetty.

(9) COVERED WAY. A wide defensive ditch, dug in 1565, allowing protected access to the coastal Redoubt.

(10) ELIZABETHAN WALLS. Sixteenth century fortifications, which incidentally have never experienced a shot in anger, are unique in the UK. Technically, as examples of defensive military engineering, they were well ahead of their time; as can be seen in the 'flankers' of King's Mount and Meg's Mount (the cannon of the time were known as 'Megs' or 'Roaring Megs') and the twin Flankers of Windmill Bastion, Brass Bastion (it housed a brass cannon) and Cumberland Bastion (after the Duke of Cumberland who passed this way to the slaughter of Culloden).

'Flankers' - inset, angled positions on the bastions that allowed cannon and musket to enfilade invaders attempting to scale the walls. They were connected by tunnels through the walls to the town, thus giving safe passage for troops and weapons.

On the Brass Bastion, by its west flanker, a section of cobbled path can be seen. The only visible remains of a sentry walkway that ran the entire length of the Walls, the whole now obscured by the grass covered mounds that were added to its defences in the seventeenth and eighteenth centuries.

The River Walk Route

Cross the bridge to Tweedmouth then turn immediately right, i.e. north and with the footpath pass beneath the Royal Tweed Bridge and swing right onto a tarmac riverbank path. After 500yds / m pass between two of the giant stone pillars supporting the main east coast railway as it sweeps majestically north over the 28 arches of the Royal Border Bridge (1). Note the small knowe left, known as 'Hang a Dyke Neuk', which carried a gallows erected in 1333 by Edward III in order to hang Berwick into submission.

Once under the arches the prepared path peters out to a thin, and in winter squelchy dirt trod, running west and south alongside the estuary wetlands of Yarrow Slake and Yarrow Haugh, home to many aquatic birds. Although narrow the trod is always distinct, as it passes Northumbrian Water's sewage works (with a revised and widened waymarked bridleway) to reach the fisherman's shelter of Toddles Shiel. From the roadway above the shieling a 'Public

Footpath' sign indicates a narrow field-side path rising gradually above the river bank. From here observe, over the silver Tweed and the rising fields, the domed and grassy top of Halidon Hill on the northern skyline (2). Continue by field fence and straggly scrub (fine nest sites for heron), to finally cross a wooden footbridge and stepped way to reach the A1(T) Berwick bypass and road bridge at the car/information park.

Join the busy road by finger post and stile, fortunately briefly, to turn right and cross the bridge over the wide Tweed. Once over, a finger post, 'Berwick 2¹/₄ miles by the Plantation', directs to a riverside pasture by a stiled and waymarked fenceside path. Pass the shelter of English New Water Shiel at the waterside, before crossing the pasture diagonally with a line of posted waymarks that funnel over a wooden footbridge and stile into the scrub and trees of the Plantation. Ascend the path and at the junction, by the northern perimeter, turn right, i.e. east, for a pleasing woodland walk before descending beneath a cluster of venerable beech to reach the riverside once more by a small cottage. Continue east with the improving path; ahead lies a giant scimitar of stone that is the Royal Border Bridge, and from the high ground to the left the remains of Berwick Castle and its ramparts (3) sweep down to the Tweed.

On the final leg, between railway bridge and modern road bridge, look out for an inscribed well prior to the clubhouse of Berwick Amateur Rowing Club - Conquerer's Well (Chalybeate), so named after Peter Conquerer, an early eighteenth century watch and clock maker in Berwick; *Chalybeate - a water containing iron.* Approaching journey's end Meg's Mount rears to the left prior to the underpass beneath the Royal Tweed Bridge leading by riverside walls to Bridge Street and Berwick Bridge.

ITEMS OF INTEREST ALONG THE WAY

(1) ROYAL BORDER BRIDGE. A high sweeping arched railway bridge of many pillars, the work of Robert Stephenson; officially declared open in August 1850 by Queen Victoria. At its northern end is Berwick Railway Station, built on the site of the ancient castle of Berwick; little remains today, although it is said many of the castle's stones now reside in the pillars of the Royal Border Bridge.

ROYAL TWEED BRIDGE. A road bridge standing between the two classics, it also received a royal opening in 1928.

(2) THE BATTLE OF HALIDON HILL. Contested in 1333, for the town of Berwick, between the bowmen of England, on the hill top, and the verve and valour of charging Scots. All day they ebbed and flowed over Halidon Hill, 'till English arrows won the day and Berwick'. Historian Lanercost states, 'The English then pursued them [The Scots] on horseback, felling them with iron-shod maces'.

(3) BERWICK FORTIFICATIONS OF EDWARD I. Work began in 1297, with gun towers added in the reign of Henry VIII, as can be seen in the massive bulwarks at the riverside and at Lord's Mount north of Brass Bastion.

Walk 30: Sandy Miles to the Pilgrim's Way

TWEEDMOUTH, COCKLAWBURN, CHESWICK SANDS to LINDISFARNE

Type of Walk:	*A linear journey, the first of several exploring and experiencing Northumberland's superb coastline, on the golden beaches that, with few exceptions, allow unhindered passage. When not on the sands the way is by coastal lanes and public paths. Infrequent waymarks make maps essential. Few coastlines match this history-soaked lordly strand for views, its plethora of sea birds and coastal vegetation.* *It is essential to check tide tables to avoid high water and ensure safe crossing times to Holy Island. This information can be found in local papers, tourist offices or noticeboards at Beal and the Causeway.*
Maps:	OS 1:25 000 Pathfinder 438, Berwick-upon-Tweed; and 452, Beal & Holy Island OS 1:50 000 Landranger Sheet 75, Berwick-upon-Tweed
Start:	Tweedmouth, at the west end of the old Berwick Bridge, GR 994526
Finish:	Holy Island village, GR 126419
Distance:	13½ miles (21.6km)
Height Gain:	82ft (25m)
Grade:	3
Walking Time:	6½-7 hours

Accommodation & Parking:
A range of accommodation available in Berwick, Tweedmouth and Spittal; also pay parking. Holy Island village has limited accommodation plus pay parking.

The Route: From the Tweedmouth side of Berwick Bridge (1) swing left, i.e. south past Tweed Dock keeping to the riverside roadway beyond the Lifeboat House and slipway. When the road fringes the sand of the Tweed estuary, home to a flotilla of swans, follow the shoreline around the broken-down fertiliser works on Sandstell Point, veering south for Spittal beach. At the southern end of Spittal promenade, with the sloping cliffs of rock classified as the Scremerston Series ahead, ascend the stepped pathway to meet the rails and electric overheads of the main east coast line. Glance behind for fine views of Berwick, its bridges and the Tweed estuary.

A gated path runs for over a mile between scarred cliffs and stone dykes, with the sounds of a restless sea, wheeling oyster-catchers and trilling larks for company, passing Toppye Knowe, The Skipper and Redshin Cove to the scatter of Sea House. On a clear day this stretch will fire the blood, for ahead the castles of Lindisfarne and Bamburgh crown the southern horizon. Beyond Sea House and its wind fashioned trees, the way is by road for a short stretch dropping beyond Saltpan Rocks to tread sand once more as Cocklawburn Beach is reached. Should high spring tides prevent a beach walk follow the roadway to its terminous and then a track over the dunes.

Cocklawburn (2) is a beach of character and much interest, the golden sand divided by a series of walkable rocky pavements spearing seawards between the varied, weathered rock of Near, Middle and Far Skerrs. Also prominent is a crumbling, but sizeable limekiln beyond Middle Skerr. Far Skerr marks the gateway to the 4 miles (6.4km) of Cheswick and Goswick Sands, totally devoid of rock except for the sculptured blackness of Cheswick Black Rocks immediately ahead.

So extensive are these sea deserts (3), at low water they seemingly stretch to Snook Point on Holy Island. **The straight line does not however provide a safe short cut and must be avoided, due to the presence of quicksands, unexploded military hardware and a racing incoming tide.** As two large grass crowned dunes standing

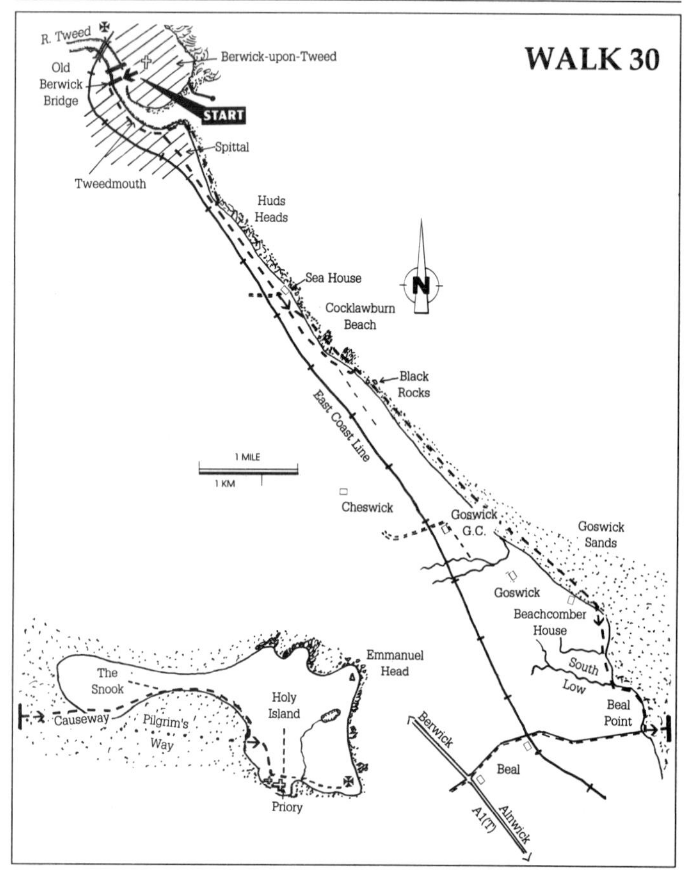

alone on the beach are reached, veer inland and hug the firm sand of the high water mark to Beachcomber House and its outbuildings. After passing a derelict World War II lookout tower leave the beach to join a public track and fertile pasture (4) path to wet and boggy South Low, with no visible crossing point (the much used sluice gate upstream traverses private property). Beal Point, and the surrounding tank trapped salt marsh are negotiated via a squelchy path to the causeway leading to Lindisfarne.

Walk east with the causeway passing the stilted refuge hut to reach the island, following the line of road east to the Chare Ends, the village and Lindisfarne priory. **Only at certain times of year, with exceptionally low tides, can the long line of sea-washed poles, marking the Pilgrim's Way, be followed to the dry land at the Chare Ends.**

For, with the flow and ebb its style
Varies from continent to isle;
Twice every day, the waves efface
Of staves and sandaled feet the trace.

Sir Walter Scott, *Marmion*, Canto 11.

ITEMS OF INTEREST ALONG THE WAY

(1) BERWICK BRIDGE, circa 1634. This fine stone arched bridge spanning the Tweed, with its sloping deck, was preceded by a stream of wooden constructions that were swept out to sea with every spring tide. It has stood the test of time, and was until 1850 the only bridge over the Tweed to Berwick.

(2) COCKLAWBURN STRATA. Visible exposed sedimentary rocks, displayed as limestone pavements and sloping beds of limestone imposed upon multi-coloured sandstones. Weathered and sea-washed into contorted shapes, Middle Skerr is pure limestone, Farr Skerr is sandstone topped with limestone and Cheswick Black Rocks are in fact red sandstone.

(3) GOSWICK SANDS. Goswick Sands, stretching north-west of Holy Island, are identified by a scatter of rotting, high poles; clearly seen at low tide from the mainland and the causeway. Erected in 1940 their purpose was to deter and prevent enemy aircraft landing on the sand flats.

(4) Local mainland farms supplied Lindisfarne Priory with provisions in centuries past.

From Goswick we've geese; from Cheswick we've cheese;
From Buckton we've ven'son in store;
From Swinhoe we've bacon, but the Scots have it taken,
And the Prior is longing for more.

Anon.

Walk 31: The Lordly Strand of Lindisfarne
THE ROUND OF INSULA SACRA - HOLY ISLAND

Type of Walk: *A short circular journey around the eastern half of Lindisfarne - or Holy Island, the northern cradle of Christianity. An island for half its life, anchored to the mainland by a causeway, it provides the walker with tranquillity amidst its sheltered dunes and invigoration along its coastline. By grassy paths, waymarked in places, to secret bays and endless dunes the walk reveals Lindisfarne priory, two of Northumberland's finest castles, the scattered Inner & Outer Farne Islands and a mass of migratory and resident birds. The Island attracts many tidal visitors, and if your desire is solitude time your walk to coincide with high water.*

It is possible to encircle the entire island, which includes a section of Lindisfarne Nature Reserve, although there are no designated rights of way for much of the journey. Please observe the local bye-laws by keeping to the designated paths. Do not tramp up and down the sensitive, unstable dunes.

Maps: OS 1:25 000 Pathfinder 452, Beal & Holy Island
OS 1:50 000 Landranger Sheet 75, Berwick-upon-Tweed

Start/Finish: Holy Island village at Lindisfarne Priory Gates, GR 126419, 5 miles (8km) E from the A1 at Beal, GR 053421.

Distance: 4 1/2 miles (7.2km)

Height Gain: Minimal

Grade: 1

Walking Time: 2-2 1/2 hours

Accommodation & Parking:
Village inns and guest houses. Public car parks (pay).

The Route: Lindisfarne Priory (1) and its twelfth century neighbouring parish church of St Mary provide the alpha and omega for this walk of concentrated delights and interest, allowing visits to both and the attached museum either before or after. From the charming village green stroll north through the narrow streets to main street, turning right past an inn and a small museum then first left at the corner of what was the well known and greatly missed Iron Rails pub. Passing north between the old curing house and the coastguard's cottages the lane reaches Robert's Farm and is reduced to a grassy track known as Straight Lonnen (2) leading for

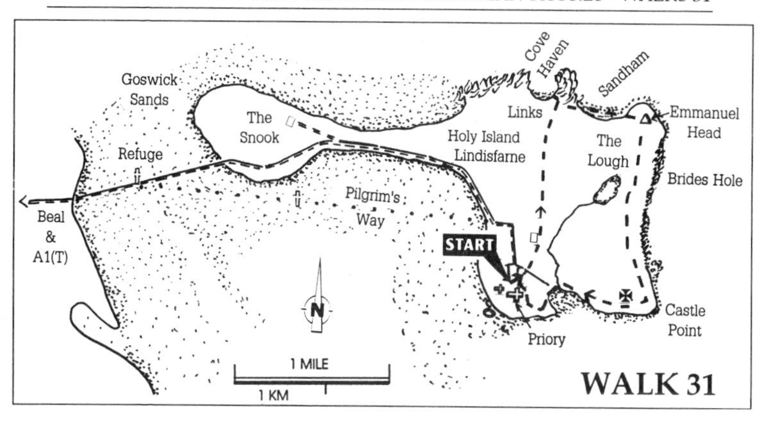

one mile to the old golf course, the Coves and Sandham Bay.

At the northern shoreline swing left for a short distance to Cove Haven, bird-washed sandstone cliffs (a rarity on the island and home to screeching sea birds) ringing the eastern end of the bay. Return east with the distinct grass path, surrounded by sea pinks and a flutter of common blue and small copper butterflies, to Sandham Bay with its golden sands and toothed reef of Keel Head, making for the prominent pyramid on Emmanuel Head (3).

This fine viewpoint, with accompanying seat, provides sightings south and east of Bamburgh Castle and the many islands of Farne. Walk, with Emmanuel Head behind us, on the grassy-shore path south for one mile, between Brides Hole and Holy Island Lough, stop-over for wintering whooper swans. Passing Sheldrake Pool and Broad Stones approach the distinctive silhouette of Lindisfarne Castle, old limekilns and three upturned coble hulls (4), above Castle Point.

It's but a step from the castle to the thin strip of sand ringing the harbour, known as The Stank, and its bobbing boats; noting to the south the twin guiding towers of The Beacons on Guile Point. Walk between water's edge and up-ended cobles, overlooked by the old herring-houses to the landward end of the jetty. Veer right rising to the small ridge known as The Heugh, here to pass through a creaking swing-gate leading by the priory wall to the Crown and Anchor and the village green.

ITEMS OF INTEREST ALONG THE WAY

I would recommend Chapter XIII of *Highways & Byways in Northumbria*, P. Anderson Graham (Macmillan, 1920) for a study of the island's history.

(1) LINDISFARNE. The Celtic Priory of Lindisfarne was founded in AD 635 by St Aidan, who later died leaning against the wooden west wall of his Bamburgh church. St Cuthbert followed and the priory continued to flourish until fired by Danish invaders in AD 875. After the Norman 'Harrying of the North' at the end of the eleventh century, Lindisfarne was 'converted' to a Benedictine Priory by Durham monks. For a full and complete story visit the English Heritage's museum and Lindisfarne Priory.

(2) LONNEN. A lane or track running between enclosed pasture or arable fields. A northern term, 'Straight Lonnen' has the Northumbrian 'e', as opposed to the two 'o's as found in Yorkshire 'lonnons'.

(3) EMMANUEL HEAD. A white beacon, standing some 30ft (9m) high, straddles this north-eastern point of the island. Its purpose is to warn shipping of the hidden reefs that surround this sector, in particular Keel Head which has in the past claimed several victims.

(4) HOLY ISLAND CASTLE, Limekilns and Coble shells. The castle, standing on a mound of basalt, is an extension of a sixteenth century harbour fort. Restored by Sir Edward Lutyens early in the 1900s, it now presents a fairy-tale profile when viewed from the harbour. The castle is open to visitors, under the stewardship of the National Trust. On the basalt/whin sill of Beblowe Crag to the east sizeable limekilns stand, kilns that used limestone from the area of Snook House, with the lime transported by colliers to Scottish ports.

The unique upturned hulls, by castle and harbourside, are the remaining skeletons of the island's once sizeable fishing fleet; put out to grass as sheds for nets, creels and equipment for today's reduced fishing boats. More than sixty cobles and several herring boats operated in the nineteenth century, as did ten pubs, and the island throbbed with the fishing, spawning many tales and ditties of the fisherfolk, such as 'Smelly Bessie and Pallid Sally'.

Twas in that place called Holy Isle
Two damsels dressed in fishwife style,
Sally was long and lean and lank

Bay Bridge over the River Derwent (Walk 25)
The giant pillars of the Royal Border Bridge (Walk 29)

Over Embleton Bay to Dunstanburgh Castle (Walk 33)
Over the Aln to Alnmouth (Walk 35)

Her shape was like a six foot plank
Her mate, fat Bess, as her name implies
Was a mass of flesh of enormous size'

Anon.

Walk 32: By Budle Sands & Bebbanbrough
BUDLE BAY, BAMBURGH to SEAHOUSES

Type of Walk: *A golden beach walk for all seasons, prevented only by tempestuous spring tides or sand-blasting gales. It offers unsurpassed views of Holy Island, Budle Bay, the splendour of Bamburgh Castle and the rocky Farne Islands. There are interests every step of the way with no ascents or navigational problems to distract, and apart from Bamburgh and Seahouses in the summer months, very few people.*

Maps: OS 1:25 000 Pathfinder 465
OS 1:50 000 Landranger Sheet 75, Berwick-upon-Tweed

Start: At the road/track junction on the B1342 by Budle, GR 156351, 3/4 mile (1.2km) NE from Waren Mill, 1 3/4 miles (2.8km) W from Bamburgh.

Finish: The Harbour, Seahouses, GR 220322

Distance: 6 3/4 miles (10.8km)

Height Gain: Minimal

Grade: 2

Walking Time: 3 hours

Accommodation & Parking:
Varied, including caravan and camping, with pay car parks at Bamburgh and Seahouses. A campsite also at Waren Mill.

The Route: From the road and track junction by Budle walk north with the sloping track, past the cottages, to Kiln Point on Budle Bay (1). At the high water mark, between the grassed-over limekilns and Lindisfarne Nature Reserve (2) notice, turn right onto the stony, shale shore. As we progress east, passing Heather Cottages, a clutch of caravans and the old jetty of an abandoned whinstone quarry above Budle Point, golden sand replaces stone. The Point, with superb views north, is marked by a lump of dolerite named Black Rock, channelling us east over rock slabs to skirt Harkess Rocks.

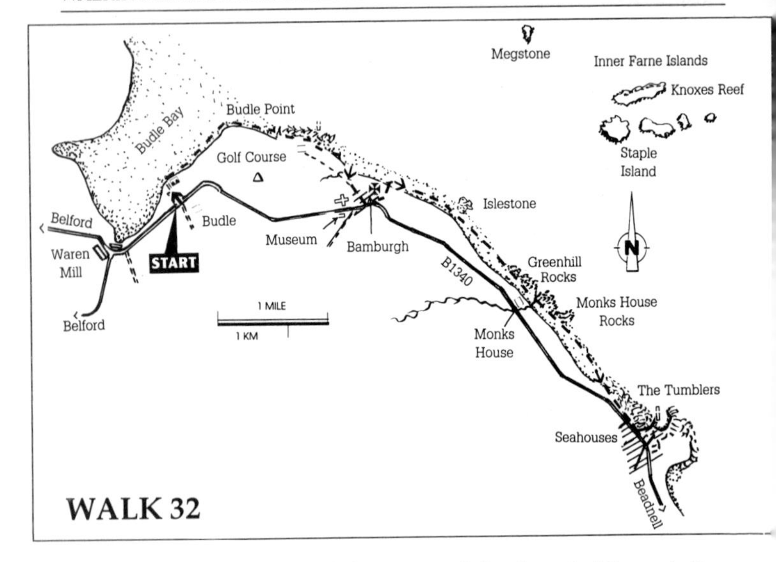

Here a cubic automated lighthouse stands by the primitive painting on Stag Rock. To the south, high on its rocky plinth, sits the most noble of all Northumberland's castles, Bamburgh Castle (3).

Continue south, passing several World War II tank traps, prior to crossing a small burn where a parking area in the dunes leads to The Wynding, south into Bamburgh (4) with its many historical attractions. Leave via the dune trods east of the castle, to the sweeping sands south-south-east to Seahouses.

The Farne Islands (5) now dominate the restless seascape, when viewed over Islestone's rocks, a favoured spot for sea birds, with the cliffs, lighthouse (white) and tower of the Inner Farne clearly visible. On the distant horizon the red and white Longstone light flashes from the Outer Farnes. Ahead, perched on the highest of the dunes, the coastguard look-out scans over the limestone of Greenhill Rocks, prior to Monks House and Monks House Rocks. Cross Brock Burn as it spreads over the sands and admire families of plump eider duck that waddle and preen at the water's edge.

With St Aidan's Dunes (a National Trust holding) on our right, leave the sands by stepped path, for the tarmac of Seahouses (6). The bustling fishing and holiday community, with arcades, fish suppers and candy floss, centres around and above its blue-boated harbour, home to the fishing fleet and the now more lucrative Farne Island tourist-trips fleet.

ITEMS OF INTEREST ALONG THE WAY

(1) BUDLE BAY. This sanctuary for resident/migratory birds, dry at low tide, except for Ross Low and Waren Burn, caught the attention of Stephen Oliver in 1835. In *Rambles in Northumberland* he mused on the relative positions of pedestrians and gentlemen.

> *The Waren can be crossed by a pedestrian, except at the time of a fresh [flood or spate], without being above the knees. It is very convenient for a pedestrian tourist who may occasionally have to wade, to wear socks in summer, which can be taken off in a moment, while a gentleman who wears long stockings up to his very fork, and who garters above the knee, has to untruss his points, and generally spends a quarter of an hour before he can uncase his legs.*

(2) LINDISFARNE NATURE RESERVE. Embraces the flats, below the high water mark, from Goswick Sands to Waren Mill, including north and western sections of Holy Island. A haven for water and sea birds, favoured by flocks of widgeon, coastal plants and insects. Note and respect the displayed bye-laws on the perimeter notice boards.

(3) BAMBURGH CASTLE. A royal residence from Saxon times, built in AD 547, on a 75ft (23m) high mass of basalt above red and white sandstone, by Ida King of Northumbria, as a wooden fort. From such royal, but simple beginnings the castle has been ravaged by Danes, rebuilt by Henry I, seiged by Border raiders and used as her own fortress by Henry VI's wife during the Wars of the Roses. Greatly battered by war and weather it was given away by James I to the Forsters, later falling by marriage into the hands of Lord Crewe, Bishop of Durham in 1704, who with great foresight began restoration and established a trust for further work in perpetuity. Today's castle owes its present appearance to W.G. Armstrong, first Baron of Cragside. It is open to the public.

(4) BAMBURGH. Named 'Bebbanbrough' by King Ida in honour of

his wife Bebba, it remains a timeless village. Visit the thirteenth century, squat stone church of St Aidan, replacing the previous wooden church established by St Aidan of Lindisfarne, against whose wall he died. A memorial to Grace Darling, the nineteenth century heroine of Bamburgh, stands outside St Aidan's. This Longstone lighthouse-keeper's daughter at the age of 23 years rescued, together with her father in September 1838, nine survivors from the *Forfarshire*, aground on Big Harcar in the Outer Farnes. Sadly Grace died from consumption four years later.

(5) FARNE ISLANDS. A bird sanctuary of international renown and favoured breeding ground for seals. Nineteen named rocky islets, outcrops of Northumberland's Great Whin Sill, make up the Inner and Outer Farnes. Centuries ago monks and holy men spent time on the Farnes; St Cuthbert, the most distinguished, retired to his cell on 'great Farn' (Inner Farne) in AD 678 but died after two months. An island with a deep cleavage at its north end, it was described by Pennant in 1769 as 'a deep chasm, from the top to the bottom of the rock, communicating with the sea, through which, in tempestuous weather, the water is forced with vast violence and noise, and forms a fine jet d'eau of sixty feet high: called the churn.'

(6) SEAHOUSES. Birth place of the obsequious kipper, the brain child of John Woodger of Seahouses who in 1843 formulated a method of 'cold smoking' herrings; the resultant inspiration he named 'kipper'.

Walk 33: Golden Beaches and a 'Turner'

BEADNELL, LOW NEWTON, DUNSTANBURGH TO CRASTER

Type of Walk: *A linear coastal journey south to the sun, encompassing the glorious sandy crescents of Beadnell Bay and Embleton Bay leading to the stark silhouettes of Dunstanburgh Castle. Endeavour to walk with low tide in order to enjoy the beaches. Alternatively public paths pass through the overlooking dunes, but do stick to the pathways as the dune ecology is fragile.*

The shoreline views are stunning, the geology interesting and the historical aspects of Beadnell and Dunstanburgh Castle engrossing, as are the wildlife of sea and shoreline.

Maps: OS 1:25 000 Pathfinder 477, Embleton & Alnmouth
OS 1:50 000 Landranger Sheet 75, Berwick-upon-Tweed
Start: Beadnell harbour, GR 237286
Finish: Craster harbour, GR 258199
Distance: 8 miles (12.8km)
Height Gain: Beach route - minimal; dunes route - 115ft (35m)
Grade: 2
Walking Time: 4 hours
Accommodation & Parking:
Hotels to caravan/camping in Beadnell, pay car park GR 235287. B/Bs and caravan parks at Craster. Park in Craster, National Trust car park - pay, GR 256198.

The Route: Walk from Beadnell's (1) tiny, often dry, harbour with its prominent and substantial limekilns, used today, as are the upturned cobles on Holy Island, for housing the fishermen's gear. So, with Beadnell Point and the harbour behind, set off south on the 2½ mile (4km) golden strand to the clearly visible rocks of Newton Point. On a good day not even the fanning waters of The Long Nanny, a substantial burn flowing in from Rosebrough Moor, will impede progress. Should tide and burn be too high the Long Nanny footbridge is at hand. As Newton Point approaches leave the sand to skirt, by waymarked path and stile, above the rock and sand displays of Snook Point and Football Hole. Leading around the communications building on the headland ease down south-west above the sloping limestone of Newton Haven to the tiny green and surrounding cottages of Low Newton by-the-Sea (2).

After perhaps a refreshment stop at Newton carry on south with the golden crescent of Embleton Bay, passing high dunes on which holiday chalets are precariously perched to cross the spread-out waters of The Skaith, fed by Embleton Burn; a footbridge is also at hand here in times of high tides. With Embleton golf course fringing the dunes and the stark outline of Dunstanburgh Castle (3) ahead we eventually leave the sands for a pathway between the now smaller and grass bound dunes and a shoreline scatter of darkened sea-worn boulders. Note the contorted limestone folds of Graymare Rock/Saddle Rock (4) as the step is quickened by the immediate presence of the Castle's remains, perched above the awesome Great

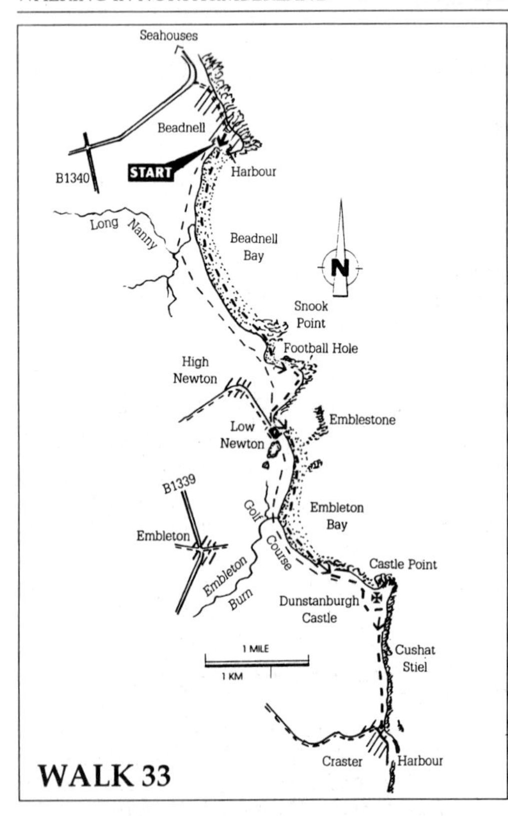

Whin Sill perpendicular cliffs (4) of Gull Crag.

Pass through a gate and gradually rise south, on what is now a pasture path, below the teetering tower of Lilburn and John of Gaunt's Gateway to swing left to the battered twin towers of The Keep. Open to the paying public the entrance is through gates to the keep; I would recommend a visit. Leave the castle with the well-beaten track south, a 1¼ mile (2km) grassy way above the shoreline rocks, much favoured by salt licking cattle, to Craster. Note the wrecked remains of a foundered trawler by the rocky point of Cushat Stiel. Appealing though Craster is (see Walk 34), you find yourself glancing back for a last look at the spiky silhouette of broken Dunstanburgh on Castle Point.

In times of high tides or adverse weather use the public paths, to Dunstanburgh, inland from the dunes. Leave Beadnell south-west, via its vast caravan park, on a duneside public path roughly parallel to the beach, passing over Long Nanny bridge and by Newton Links House to the craggy

Dunstanburgh Castle

rocks above Newton-by-the-Sea. Leave Newton behind the Ship Inn. Passing between Newton Pool's bird hides and the holiday chalets skirt several holes of Embleton golf course to cross The Skaith footbridge. Beyond, the club house is passed and the public path treks alongside the outward holes to Saddle Rock and Dunstanburgh Castle.

ITEMS OF INTEREST ALONG THE WAY

(1) BEADNELL. Site of St Ebba's Chapel on the point, this original fishing village, with eighteenth century quayside lime kilns, is now distended beyond recognition by a surfeit of caravan parks.

(2) LOW NEWTON-BY-THE-SEA. A tight cluster of cottages crouching by the sands of Newton Haven, surrounded by a clutch of sailing dinghys and surfboards, all straining to join the colourful cobles bobbing in the lee of rocky Emblestone. Behind the hamlet is Newton Pool nature reserve and bird sanctuary.

(3) DUNSTANBURGH CASTLE. The suffix 'burgh' suggests an Anglo-Saxon connection, the rocky point settled perhaps by sea-borne invaders. Apparently not, for it was not until the early 1300s that a fortress was built on lonely exposed Gull Crag by Thomas, Earl of Lancaster, later executed for treason on orders from Edward II. Succeeding keepers of the castle increased the fortifications, with the Lilburn Tower c.1325 by Sir John Lilburn, and the sealed up twin towered Keep and John o'Gaunt's Gateway c.1380 by A Warden of the Marches, Sir John of Gaunt. There is little more to tell, except it played host to both sides during the Wars of the Roses and achieved its present condition from neglect and winter storms, rather than the cannon of Yorkist and Lancastrian. In a cove below the castle, there are quartz crystals, known locally as 'Dunstanburgh Diamonds'.

(4) SADDLE ROCK and GULL CRAG. Folklore has it that arched Saddle Rock was the result of two rushing streams of magma colliding. Gull Crag, rising 100ft (30m) above the pounding sea is a cliff of basaltic columns, resembling the Giant's Causeway and the delights of Fingle's Cave. Within the rocks of the Crag is Rumble Churn, an upright chasm in the basalt, into which the North Sea surges producing a tremendous rumble and frequent castle-high water spouts.

Walk 34: The Craster Round
CRASTER, LONGHOUGHTON TO RUMBLING KERN

Type of Walk: *A gentle, yet in its way spectacular, Northumbrian journey of two definite halves. The first is a pastoral experience by marked field paths and country lanes passing the fine house and gardens of Howick Hall. The second leg traverses waymarked cliff and shoreline paths, exhibiting sea and coastal-scapes with an abundance of seashore wildlife and unique exposed strata.*

Maps: OS 1:25 000 Pathfinder 477, Embleton & Alnmouth
OS 1:50 000 Landranger Sheet 81, Alnwick & Morpeth

Start/Finish: Craster, National Trust car park, GR 256198

Distance: 7$^{3}/_{4}$ miles (12.4km)

Height Gain: 213ft (65m)

Grade: 2

Walking Time: 3$^{1}/_{2}$ hours

Accommodation & Parking:
B/Bs and caravan parks at Craster and Longhoughton.
Park in Craster, National Trust car park (pay), GR 256198.

The Route: Leave the spacious car park by a side gate east, walking into the village on a gravel path and with the first right past a small boat or two walk south on a grass path behind a row of houses. At the waymarked gate swing right with the field perimeter to the gorse covered Howick Scar. Rising west over this west-sided rocky outcrop on a stony dirt track descend through a cutting, past two monkey puzzle trees (1), into and through the gated yard of Howick Scar Farm. *Please ensure that all gates are closed.* Cross the road and with the cart track rise west-south-west to reach the northern tip of a second west facing crag, Hips Heugh, crossing two ladder stiles en route. To the north Craster Tower, first recorded in 1415, hides among the trees.

The public path skirts the rocky face of Hips Heugh, then by stile and southbound waymarked field path, past a tree encircled cricket ground, reaches by an ascending track the entrance and gardens of Howick Hall (2). At the Hall entrance continue south by road, descending to pass beneath a footbridge and cross the attractive dene of Howick Burn. Swing south-west, on roadside verges where possible, through a pleasing selection of venerable broadleaves (the

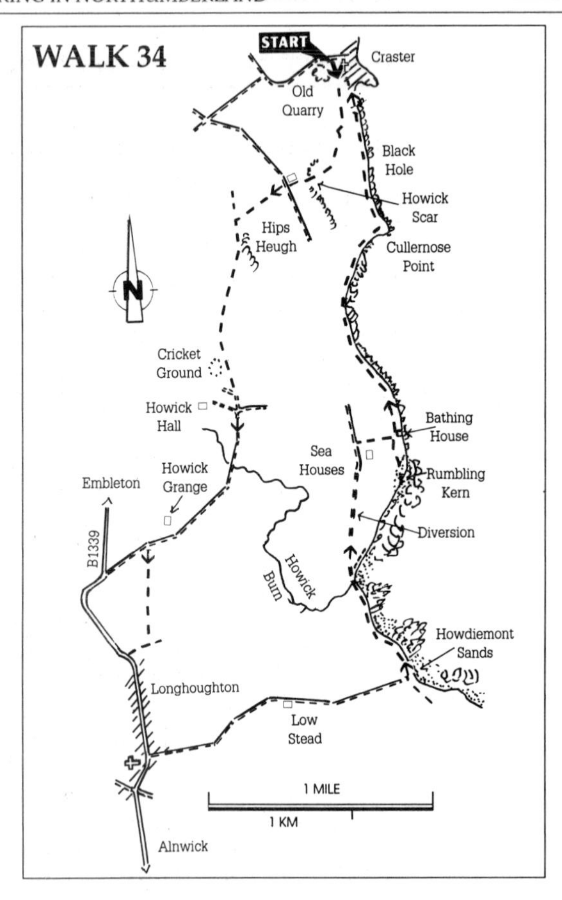

only virtue of this section), for a further 2/3 mile (1km) to just beyond the entrance to Howick Grange. On the left a wicket gate opens onto a cart track south, through three fields, leading via a shelter strip to the north end of Longhoughton (3). A long village today it houses the personnel of RAF Boulmer, base of the Sea and Mountain Search and Rescue Squadron, to whom some walkers and mountaineers have cause to be eternally grateful.

Cullernose Bay and Point

Leave the village by turning left, i.e. east opposite the squat Norman church for a $1^{1}/_{2}$ mile (2.4km) lane walk, past the tidy buildings of Low Stead, to the gate and emergency telephone above Howdiemont Sands. Here begin $3^{1}/_{4}$ miles (5.2km) north on one of the most varied sections of Northumberland's seaboard; by sandy, rocky coves and cliffs, that although not high, are of great geological interest. Never dull, they are broken by small havens and inlets known locally as 'kerns/churns'.

Sand and grass clad low cliffs lead to Iron Scars as the picturesque Howick Burn Mouth is passed by an arched footbridge. Once across, *do not follow the shoreline public path to Rumbling Kern as it is closed due to cliff erosion;* take the alternative farm track beyond Sea Houses Farm turning right to rejoin the coast path at 'The Bathing House' above the stacs and beaches by Rumbling Kern (4). Carry on north on the marked path, through clumps of windswept blackthorn, as it follows the cliff's indentations, revealing at low tide spectacular rock formations. Creations ranging from the folds of sedimentary limestones with yellow sandstones above, through the sea washed boulders of whinstone to the columns of hard dolerite make up bird-washed Cullernose Point (5).

Skirt around the point, the fine grass path running just above the slab pavement high water mark, passing Black Hole and skipping by Hole o' the Dike as Craster (6) hoves into view, and even more dramatically the battered profile of Dunstanburgh Castle astride Castle Point. Pass by the children's playground, the Jolly Fisherman and the renowned Craster Kipper House to reach Craster's quiet natural harbour. It's but a short stroll west to the car park.

ITEMS OF INTEREST ALONG THE WAY

(1) MONKEY PUZZLES. Trees, it is said, indicating in times past that a blacksmith's shop stood nearby. As to why I know not.

(2) HOWICK HALL. Built in 1782, this fine Georgian mansion with extensive gardens, was the seat of Earl Grey, promoter of the Reform Bill. If time permits visit the gardens and the woodland walk, open to the public on spring and summer afternoons.

(3) LONGHOUGHTON. This solid low church, restored in 1873, displays a defensive square castellated tower and retains its Norman nave and chancel arch.

(4) RUMBLING KERN. A rock barrel through which the tides noisily ebb and flow into a large rock pool; some distance below are the weather sculptured stones of 'The Bathing House'. Built for the Greys of Howick Hall, and later used as a fisherman's house, it stands abandoned and silent.

(5) CULLERNOSE POINT. The point where the dolerite extrusions of Long Heugh slope into the sea, illustrating the geological skeleton of this stretch of coastline.

(6) CRASTER. Its sheltered harbour, a rarity along this coastline, was used to transport much of the whinstone quarried around Craster. The car park was once a whinstone quarry. Today the fishing is on the decline; not so the thriving and tasty Craster kipper.

Walk 35: A Medieval Port, Auric Sands and Warkworth
ALNMOUTH to WARKWORTH

Type of Walk: *A mixture of town and pastoral river-mouth walking, connected by the glorious strand of Northumberland's beaches. A leisurely linear coastal walk, the most southerly in this guide, of intriguing interest by lane, public pathways and golden sand that provides long remembered views. The journey can be shortened by 3¾ miles (6km) with a beach crossing of the outflow of the Aln. This is possible for three-quarters of an hour either side of low water.*

Maps: OS 1:50 000 Landranger 81, Alnwick, Morpeth

Start: Alnmouth Village Golf Clubhouse, GR 248104

Finish: Warkworth Castle, GR 246057

Distance: 9¼ miles (14.8km). **Shorter Walk** 5½ miles (8.8km)

Height Gain: 262ft (80m). **Shorter Walk** 82ft (25m)

Grade: 2

Walking Time: 4½ hours. **Shorter Walk** 2½ hours.

Accommodation & Parking:
Available in Alnmouth and Warkworth. Parking: Alnmouth at GR 251107 alongside the village golf course; Warkworth at the dunes car park, GR 254064, and/or by church and riverside.

The Route: The Golf Clubhouse of Alnmouth (1) is our starting point for this invigorating village and coast-line walk. Walk north through Alnmouth, via Northumberland Street, to the roundabout signposted Foxton/Boulmer. Continue north past Alnmouth Board School to just beyond the entrance of Mount Pleasant. Here drop left to a stepped stile leading through a bank of scrubby gorse and scrub above the River Aln. Leave the scrub north for a stepped fence stile, then descend sharp left to the river.

A distinct riverside path winds west, flanked by tall grasses, waterside flora and home to aquatic birds, including swans. Carry on south-west beyond the gorse, then leaving the river cross an arable field by narrow trod to Hawthorn Cottage, Lesbury. Turn left through the village, passing the Norman church of St Mary's, Lesbury and the Coach Inn to a junction with the A1068. Swing left to the pathless bridge over the Aln, crossing with care and some alacrity, then via a raised footpath south to Curly Lane.

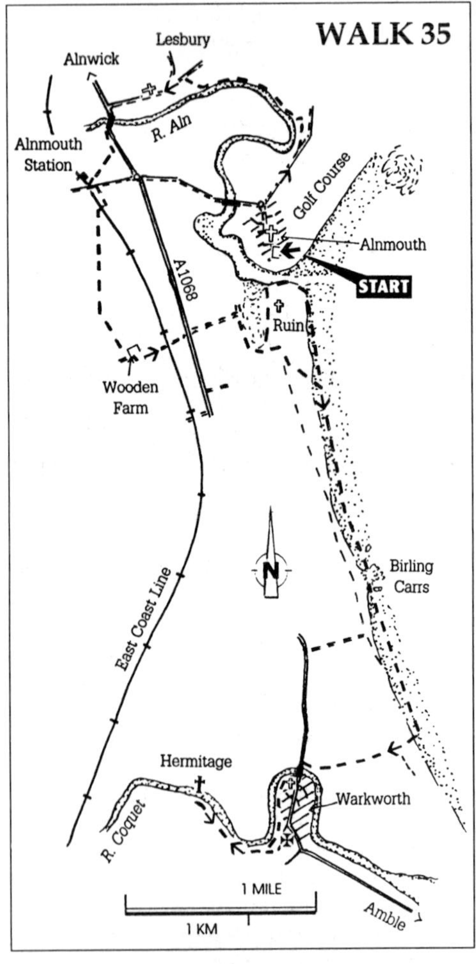

Veer right rising to Alnmouth station entrance, then turn left for 70yds/m to the bridleway sign 'Wooden Farm 1 mile'. By a children's playground, pastures and an archway under the east coast railway line, diagonally cross (south) the right shoulder of the pasture brow ahead. Once over and through the corner gate progress south, with eye-catching views of Alnmouth village and the Aln estuary, alongside a post and wire fence, through wicket gates, to Wooden Farm. Once through the gated farmyard turn left by cottages and farm, east, to cross the rail line and the A1068.

Descend the surfaced lane, 'Waterside House 1/2 mile', to where the lane angles left, leaving it right for a fieldside bridleway south to a rough dune bound track. From this point the beach can be

Warkworth Castle in springtime

accessed, north by Church Hill with its Saxon cross and old Norman arch, or south through the dunes.

$2^{1/2}$ miles (4km) of beach walking at its best over the auric sands, broken only by the sea-washed rocks of Birling Carrs, take us ever closer to the white lighthouse on Coquet Island, the darkened finger of Amble's breakwater, and the hidden approaches of Warkworth. 1 mile (1.6km) south of Birling Carrs look out for the solitary lifebelt marking a sandy track through the dunes leading by stepped way through Warkworth's dunes car park to Coquet's picturesque medieval bridge (2) and the timeless charm of Warkworth.

Turn right onto a riverside walkway passing by the spired church of St Lawrence (3) alongside the tranquil Coquet, lined with stately sycamore, ash and beech, so different from the white waters met in Upper Coquetdale (Walk 9). Continue, as directed by frequent signposts, beneath the dramatic outlines of Warkworth Castle (4), touched by time and the hand of man, en route to the rocky confines of Warkworth's Hermitage (5). Return along the riverside rising right to browse around the jewel in Warkworth's crown, the castle of Harry Hotspur.

ITEMS OF INTEREST ALONG THE WAY

(1) ALNMOUTH. Founded in the twelfth century by de Vesci, Lord of Alnwick, it became a borough in 1174, trading as a market and port. During medieval times its importance as a grain port grew, as did its quayside granaries; remains of these high buildings can be seen on the landward side of the town. Alnmouth's metamorphosis to a residential holiday town began in 1806, when a violent winter's storm gouged a new channel to the sea, cutting off Church Hill from the town thus ending its port facilities.

(2) COQUET BRIDGE. This fourteenth century bridge, a scheduled ancient monument spanning the Coquet, replaced an earlier stone arched bridge on the same site. Its sloping deck cobbled with dolerite bears an archway and fortified tower at its southern end. The author can remember driving across this bridge in the early 1960s.

(3) CHURCH OF ST LAWRENCE. Saxon in origin, now fashioned by Norman church builders (not its spire), it suffered from incursions north of the border, 1174 being the year of mass slaughter of townsfolk sheltering within its walls.

(4) WARKWORTH CASTLE. A fortified site since early in the twelfth century growing in stature and strength under the Percys; a bulwark against the Scots and a symbol of the House of Percy. As with many of the county's castles Warkworth has been cast down only to rise again, restored by the Percys, Dukes of Northumberland in the eighteenth century. Today's castle is open to the public under the stewardship of English Heritage.

(5) THE HERMITAGE. Carved into the outcrop rock of the northern riverbank is a small chapel cell, sleeping quarters and a confessional. Speculation is rife as to the origins of this cell behind the inscribed door lintel Latin reputed to read 'My Tears Have Been My Meat Day And Night'. Visits can be made by ferry from Easter until 30 September, Wednesday and Sunday 11am to 5pm.

LONG DISTANCE WALKS

Several, in fact quite a few, national / regional long distance trail and walk routes either pass through, finish in, or are contained within Northumberland. Two, The Pennine Way and St Cuthbert's Way, are officially recognized and therefore waymarked, the remainder are devised by and/or recorded by individuals utilising public paths and bridleways or permissive paths. Those listed below include the majority of the better known/publicised trails, the inclusion of which and of those not mentioned, does not in any way classify or prejudge the merits of any long distance walks associated with Northumberland.

The Pennine Way: England's first official long distance path, c.1964, from Edale, Derbyshire to Kirk Yetholm in the Scottish Borders, journeys north for 79 waymarked miles (126km) through the wilds of Northumberland for its penultimate and most testing stage. Wisely accompanying the River South Tyne into the county and thence with the ups and downs of Hadrian's Roman Wall, it then plods through Wark Forest and by Shitlington Crags to the frontier township of Bellingham nestling by the River North Tyne. Beyond, monotonous moorland and forest ways lead to Byrness in Redesdale and onto the Cheviot range for a scenic high-level trek of 25 miles (40km) - plus 2 miles if the detour to Cheviot's summit is included - along the Border Line.

St Cuthbert's Way: This recent 62½ mile (100km) cross border route (for walkers only) travels from Melrose Abbey, where St Cuthbert started his ministry, to Lindisfarne Priory, where he became prior. It enters Northumberland through the Cheviot Hills, crossing the border line between White Swire and Eccles Cairn. From this point the varied and picturesque waymarked (a Celtic cross) way winds for 30½ miles (48.8km) to Lindisfarne (Holy Island). It passes en route through the high prairies of the eastern Cheviots, Wooler and Weetwood Moor then through the River Till valley, for an airy agrarian route north over the outcrop crags by St Cuthbert's cave to Fenwick, and the coastal flatlands leading to the island causeway and Lindisfarne Priory.

Hadrian's Wall Walk: A walk with the Wall, from Wallsend, Tyneside west to Bowness-on-Solway, Cumbria, devised and described by Mark Richards in 1993, and as such the route carries no official status nor specific waymarks. The section through Northumberland covers some 50 miles (80km) and contains not only the most complete remains of the Wall with adjoining encampments, forts, milecastles and turrets, but also covers the dramatically scenic sections of the north-facing Great Whin Sill crags including Sewingshields Crags, Highshield Crags and Peel Crags. A stimulating journey through time that will educate and invigorate. (The proposed national trail, 'Hadrian's Wall Path', is at the time of writing in its feasibility and consultation stages and I have been informed that it appears unlikely to receive its 'National Trail' status for at least five years.)

The Alternative Pennine Way: Designed by Dennis Brook & Phil Hinchliffe in 1992 this Way treks, by more gentle and perhaps picturesque ways, from Ashbourne, Derbyshire to its conclusion in the rugby and abbey Tweedside town of Melrose. It covers 55 miles (88km) as it journeys through Northumberland from its entry point into West Allen Dale, taking in Allenheads, Haltwhistle, Hadrian's Wall, vast tracts of Kielder Forest leading to Byrness, prior to exiting from Coquet Head to the Scottish Borders.

Lakeland to Lindisfarne: A recent 190 mile (304km) coast to coast trek from Ravenglass in the Lake District to Northumberland's Holy Island of Lindisfarne. Not a designated long distance path, this creation of John Gillham slips into the county by the 'blackdoor' of wild West Allen Dale at Coalcleugh for its 119 mile (190km) journey to the golden crossing to Lindisfarne. It embraces and enjoys along the way the abbey and market town of Hexham, North Tynedale and Redesdale to the great sandstone crags of Simonside above Coquetdale. Here we are given a choice of routes to the coast, one a moorland/pastoral way via the county town of Alnwick to Alnmouth then north on the heritage coast to Lindisfarne. or for those with energy to spare by picturesque and historic Coquetdale for an eastern loop of the Cheviot range, including Muckle Cheviot, then to Wooler, Belford and Lindisfarne.

An Alternative Coast to Coast: This particular coast to coast from

Walney Island by Barrow-in-Furness, composed by Dennis Brook & Phil Hinchliffe, enters Northumberland via the Carrier's Way over Mohope Moor leading into West Allen Dale. Its north and north-eastern progress (with several alternative detours) encompasses terrain that is uniquely Northumbrian, ranging from the lead dales of Allen through Tynedale's Hexham, Wark and Redesmouth to the delights of Coquetdale, prior to a high level traverse of the Cheviot Hills and onto the crags and coastal pastures that signal the causeway crossing to Holy Island. In total 84 miles (134km) on Northumbrian soil.

The Reiver's Way: A walk of 150 miles (240km), entirely within Northumberland, that is not an officially recognized long distance path but the creation of Ken Coulson, first described by H.O. Wade and packaged in 1993 as *The Reiver's Way* by James Roberts. It winds and wanders, basically north, through the varied landscapes and histories of Northumberland from Corbridge to Allendale, crossing the River South Tyne and Hadrian's Wall prior to the dour moors to Elsdon. Here the trees of Harwood lead to the conspicuous crags of Simonside, Rothbury and delightful Coquetdale then onward by Clennell Street to the heavens or hell of the Cheviot Hills, through which, by some fairly serious walking, Wooler is reached. Then by a choice of routes to the coast at Budle Bay for a fine trek south with the shore line (if the tide is out) to Craster for a final split leg to Alnwick.

GLOSSARY OF NAMES & LOCAL TERMS

Abidings	Dwelling, medieval
Auld	Old
Auric	Golden
Aye	For ever/always
Bastle	Defensive farmhouse
Bell	Hill
Bield	Shelter, from the elements
Blaeberry	Bilberry, small edible purple berry
Blaws	Blows
Brae	Bank
Brig	Bridge
Burn	Upland stream
Cadger	Hawker or carter
Cairn	Stone marker, on boundary/route/burial chamber
Callit	Called
Canny	Good/fine
Capstone	Stone or stones covering burial chamber/drystone walls
Carrier	Packhorse man
Caste doune	Thrown down/demolished
Chatter	Hardcore/small stone packing in drystone walls
Cist	Stone burial box
Clarts/clarty	Dirt/mud - dirty/muddy
Cleugh	Narrow cleft or gully with watercourse
Coble	Fishing boat (Northumbrian design) with sail/engine
Col	Upland saddle between two summits
Collie	Sheep dog
Corstopitum	Roman encampment
Crag	Cliff or rocky outcrop
Currick	Stone shelters or cairns
Cushat	Wood pidgeon

Dene/dean	Small tree-lined gorge with burn
Dod	Flat domed hilltop
Donalds	Mountains, 2000-2500ft, listed by Percy Donald
Dour	Dull/obstinate
Drift	Mine entrance into a hillside
Droon	Drown
Drover	Herdsman who walked stock to market
Dyke/dike	Drystone wall or man-made ditch
Dyvers	Diverse
Fain	Glad/joyful
Feral	Semi-wild goat descended from farm stock
Flue	Stone/earth extraction tunnel from lead smelt mill
Galena	Lead ore
Galloways	Packhorses carrying lead ore for the carriers
Gill	North Pennine burn
Gimmer	Female sheep
Glebe	Church land/field
Glidders	Scree
Grange	Abbey/monastery farm
Hag	Gully of exposed peat, invariably saturated
Haugh	Flat pasture/land by river or burnside
Heid	Head
Heugh	Sharp ended low hill
Hope	Shelter below ground/valley
Hoy	Throw/toss
Hush	Water-scoured gully exposing lead veins
Incline	Sloping waggon-way for transporting coal/lead
Kern/churn	Channels/inlets eroded by sea and rolling rocks in coastal strata
Knowe	Small hill/shoulder
Law	Hill
Level	Lead mine entrance/tunnel
Linn	Waterfall/cascade
Longhouse	Single storey farmhouse housing farmer/animals

Lonnen	Farm / cart track between fences / walls
Lough	Small lake
Midden	Heap of ashes / dung
Mire/moss	Wet boggy ground, often source of burn
Muckle	Large / great
Nae	No
Nolt	Cattle
Peewit	Plover / lapwing
Pele/peel	Defensive fortified tower of clan / family chieftain
Peth	Path / pathway, medieval
Pike	Hilltop / summit
Port	Passage
Quhilk	Which
Ranters	Primitive Methodists
Reiver	Cattle thief / blackmailer or mosstrooper
Resetter	Fence / receiver of stolen goods
Ride	Fire breaks between conifer stands
Rigg	Ridge of high ground
Rodes	Medieval tracks / roads
Sae	So
Salter	Carriers of salt
Saughey	Sighing / lamenting
Scotsman's Heid	Cotton grass, grows on wet uplands
Shaws	Thickets
Sheen	Bright / shining
Shieling	High level stone shelter / house
Sike/syke	Burn / stream
Skerr	Fingers of outcropping seashore strata
Skew arched	Twisted / off-set arch
Smelt/smelting	Extraction of metals (lead / silver) by heat
Smout	Hole in stone wall for passage of sheep
Soughing	Sighing / whispering
Spang	Bounced / spun
Spate	Rushing torrent / flood
Spout	Waterfall / linn / cascade
Stane	Stone
Steading	Farm buildings

Stell	Stone sheep shelter, on high ground invariably round to prevent snow drifting
Strand	Beach of the sea
Swire	Lower ground between two hills, allowing passage
Thin	When referring to wind cold / cutting
Thruft/thruff	Binding stone in drystone wall
Trod	Thin often ill-defined upland path
Trows	Small valleys
Tup	Ram / entire male sheep
Washing	Grading and cleaning of lead ore with water
Wether/wedder	Castrated ram / tup
Whaup	Curlew

BIBLIOGRAPHY

The Alternative Coast to Coast, D. Brook & P. Hinchliffe (Cicerone Press,1996)

The Alternative Pennine Way, D. Brook & P. Hinchliffe (Cicerone Press, 1992)

Best Walks in Northumberland, Frank Duerden (Constable & Co, 1990)

Comprehensive Guide to Northumberland, W.W. Tomlinson (David & Charles, 1989)

Upper Coquetdale, David Dippie Dixon (Robert Redpath, 1904)

Exploring Northumbria, George Collard (Alan Sutton Publishing,1988)

Hadrian's Wall, Vol 1: The Wall Walk, Mark Richards (Cicerone Press, 1993)

Hadrian's Wall, Vol 2: Wall Country Walks, Mark Richards (Cicerone Press, 1996)

Highways & Byeways in Northumbria, P.A. Graham (Macmillan & Co, 1920)

A History of Lead Mining in the Pennines, A. Raistrick and B. Jennings (The Northern Mines Research Society, 1965)

Kielder Country Walks, Alan Hall (Questa Publishing 1995)

The King's England - Northumberland, Arthur Mee (Hodder & Stoughton, 1964)

Lakeland to Lindisfarne, John Gillham (Crowood Press, 1995, paperback 1996)

National Park Guide, No.7 'Northumberland' (HMSO, 1969)

Northumbria in the Days of Bede, P. Hunter Blair (V. Gollancz, 1976)

Northumbria Walks, Ordnance Survey Pathfinder Guide (Jarrold Publishing, 1991)

Northumbrian Coastline, Ian Smith (Sandhill Press, 1988)

Northumbrian Heritage, N. Ridley (Robert Hale, 1968)

Northumberland National Guide, Tony Hopkins (Webb & Bower) (Michael Joseph, 1987)

The Northumberland Landscape, Robert Newton (Hodder & Stoughton, 1972)

North Pennines, Alan Hall (Dalesman Publishing Company, 1996)

Portrait of Northumberland, Nancy Ridley (Robert Hale, 1965)

Rambles in Northumberland and The Scottish Border, Stephen Oliver the Younger (Frank Graham, Newcastle-upon-Tyne, 1st edition 1835)

The Reiver's Way Northumberland, James Roberts (Cicerone Press, 1993)

St Cuthbert's Way, Roger Smith & Ron Shaw (designed by Scottish Borders Council)

Plankey Mill Suspension Bridge (Walk 22)

USEFUL INFORMATION

Northumberland National Park

Recreation and Visitors, Eastburn, South Park, Hexham
NE46 1BS (01434) 605555

NATIONAL PARK CENTRES

Once Brewed (Southern Area), The Military Road
(01434) 344396

Rothbury (Central Area), Church House
(01669) 620887

Ingram (Northern Area), The Old School House
(01665) 578248

Forestry Commission

Environmental Officer, Ealsburn, Bellingham NE48 2AH
(01434) 220242

Recreation Forester, Kielder District, Ealsburn, Bellingham
NE48 2AH (01434) 220242

Kielder Castle Visitor Centre, Kielder Village
(01434) 250209

Rothbury Forest District, 1 Walby Hill, Rothbury NE65 7NT
(01669) 620569

Northumbrian Water

Recreation and Conservation Officer, Abbey Road, Pity Me,
Durham DH1 5FJ (0191) 383 2222

Visitor Centre, Tower Knowe, Falstone NE48 1BX
(01434) 240398

Leaplish Waterside Park, Kielder Water, Falstone NE48 1BX
(01434) 250312

Northumbria Tourist Board

Head Office, Aykley Heads, Durham DH1 5UX
(0191) 384 6905

TOURIST INFORMATION CENTRES

The Shambles, Alnwick NE66 1TN (01665) 510665
Dilston Terrace, Amble NE65 0DT (01665) 712313
Aderstone Services, Aderstone, Belford NE70 7JU (01668) 213678
Main Street, Bellingham NE48 2BH (01434) 220616
Castlegate, Berwick-upon-Tweed TD15 1JS (01289) 330733
Hill Street, Corbridge NE45 5AA (01434) 632815
Church Hall, Main Street, Haltwhistle NE49 0BE (01434) 322002
The Manor Office, Hallgate, Hexham NE46 1XD (01434) 605225
Tower Knowe, Kielder Water NE48 1BX (01434) 240398
The Chantry, Bridge Street, Morpeth NE61 1PJ (01670) 511323
Military Road, Bardon Mill, Once Brewed NE47 7AN (01434) 344396
Church House, Church Street, Rothbury NE65 7UP (01669) 620887
Seafield Road Car Park, Seahouses NE68 7SR (01665) 721436
Bus Station Car Park, High Street, Wooler NE71 6LD (01668) 282123

National Trust

Regional Office, Scots Gap, Morpeth NE61 4EG (01670) 774691

Nature Conservancy Council

Regional Office, Archbold House, Archbold Terrace, Newcastle-upon-Tyne NE2 1EG (0191) 281 6316/7

English Heritage

Northern Area - Newcastle (0191) 261 1585
- Carlisle (01228) 31777

Northumberland County Council Countryside Service

County Hall, Morpeth NE61 2EF (01670) 533000

Rights of Way Officers, County Hall, Morpeth NE61 2EF (01670) 534084
County Archaeologist, County Hall, Morpeth NE61 2EF (01670) 533000

Otterburn Range Liaison Officer
MOD Otterburn Training Area, Otterburn NE19 1NX
(0191) 261 1046
Range Control Officer (01830) 520569

Youth Hostels Association (England and Wales)
North Regional Office, PO Box 11, Matlock DE4 2XA
(01629) 825850
Area Office, Bowey House, William Street,
Newcastle-upon-Tyne NE3 1SA (0191) 284 7473

Scottish Youth Hostels Association
7 Glebe Crescent, Stirling FK8 2JA (01786) 891400

Northumberland Wildlife Trust
The Hancock Museum, Newcastle-upon-Tyne NE2 4PT
(0191) 232 0038

Ordnance Survey Office
Ordnance Survey, Romsey Road, Maybush, Southampton
SO9 4DH (01703) 792000

Weather Forecasts
Newcastle Meteorological Office, Newcastle Weather Centre
(0191) 232 6453
Weather Call 7 Day Regional Forecast, North-east England
(01891) 112261
Metro Radio Daily Forecast: FM - 91.7, AM - 1152
Radio Newcastle Daily Forecast: FM - 95.4 & 96.0, AM - 1458
Tyne Tees Television Daily Forecast: Channel 3 and Teletext (Regional Forecast)